Growing Up Black
in Rural Mississippi

Growing Up Black

in Rural Mississippi

Memories of a Family,
Heritage of a Place

CHALMERS ARCHER, JR.

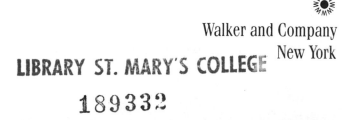

Walker and Company
New York

First published in the United States of America in 1992 by Walker Publishing Company, Inc.

Published simultaneously in Canada by Thomas Allen & Son Canada, Limited, Markham, Ontario

Library of Congress Cataloging-in-Publication Data
Archer, Chalmers, 1928–
    Growing up Black in rural Mississippi / by Chalmers Archer, Jr..
        p.   cm.
    Includes index.
    ISBN 0-8027-1175-8
        1. Afro-Americans—Mississippi—Holmes County—Biography.
    2. Archer family.   3. Holmes County (Miss.)—Biography.   4. Holmes
    County (Miss.)—Rural conditions.   5. Archer, Chalmers, 1928–
    —Childhood and youth.   I. Title.
    F347.H6A73   1992
    976.2'62500496073022—dc20
        [B]   91-30206
                                                                    CIP

Book design and illustrations by Shelli Rosen

Printed in the United States of America

10   9   8   7   6   5   4   3   2   1

Dedicated to
my father, "Mr. Chat,"
and my mother, "Miss Eva"

Contents

Preface
ix

Acknowledgments
xv

Prologue: Grandpa Payton's Initiation
1

1 The Place
3

2 Moving On
13

3 Conversations with Papa
19

4 Uncle Nick
29

5 A Poor Black Farm Kid
41

6 Church and Plow, Bullets and Hope
61

7 Our Aunt Mama Jane
73

8 Tales of Birth and Death
87

9 A Sense of Community
101

10 On Education (and Mama)
111

11 Black/White
124

12 The Young Exile
140

Appendix: Helpful Resources for
Research on Black American History
149

Index
153

Preface

Before you read on, let me tell you just a few things about this period in my life, in the lives of my family and extended family, and about this book. What went on around our family, what happened to us, and what went on within ourselves touched on many environments. The plantation next to our farm. The town of Tchula. The religious community; the countryside; Lexington, Mississippi, itself; and all of America.

Growing Up Black in Rural Mississippi is a book drawn from the memories of an extended family. The Archer family. A family that experienced the rural South. It is about the times and trials of a people who struggled for survival in an era of social extremes. It is about the good and the bad of mainly two decades, the 1930s and 1940s, but also draws on black experiences prior to that time and key events after 1955. This biography and family history is intended to communicate, firsthand, episodes from our Mississippi heritage. It is intended to fill a gap in black history. These selections of experiences will, I hope, intrigue scholars, general readers, researchers, and all students of American history. The goal of this book is to provide a useful picture of a past period of rural life and of a particular people in the South. This book is about some who are no longer with us but who told their experiences to others. It is "spoken" history. It is a living memory of experiences, an oral heritage of black people who actually lived and many who are still living a particular way of life.

It is a book about farmers, teachers, preachers, cooks, quiltmakers, and convicts. About black landowners and tenants. About education and health conditions and recreation. And making a living. It is intended to demonstrate the diversity of life-styles and social practices of a black society. I wanted to show how, although our external environment was controlled, our internal environment, culture, and values were maintained. Black history is a cumulative legacy of people's past migrations, life-styles of families, idiosyncrasies of past leaders, changing economic and legal situations, and social mores.

Growing Up Black in Rural Mississippi tells of agriculture and black rural life. It is about crops and garden patches and country stores. It's about plantations, boll weevils, and a cotton culture. It is about simple, everyday things. Trips to cotton gins. Drinking gourds and cisterns and springs and wells. Creeks, streams, and the Mississippi River. Bad roads, mud, corn, and religion. The book's events include buggy rides and ghost stories and southern myths.

And it is about those times when courage and dreams outweighed fears. Those were times of strong faith, of deeply loving one another, of unifying forces such as the church and the family.

In those years black people had to take advantage of any small opportunity. To make the best of bad situations. To learn to make their own future regardless of odds. And to hold on to the belief that someday they would become partners in the American dream, with equal justice for all. All the while, many black people led terrible lives on the plantations and went into involuntary servitude for debts. This book tells how Tchula, Mississippi, and Lexington, Mississippi, used to be. Of a sad but sometimes happy time in American black history.

This book presents families with what might seem a curious claim to recorded history. By all rules of schoolbook history, these are ordinary people. They commanded no armies, ruled no empires, took no part in major history-making decisions. A few of them achieved renown, but none was ever a national hero. None was ever a national villain either. Yet what they were able to do, along with thousands of others just like them, was more decisive for American history than many acts of statesmen who basked in brighter glory.

What this family and community did was more important than the shuttling of armies back and forth across frontiers. The folks in Tchula effected more power for good and bad than numerous decrees of presidents and legislatures. Those families were and are a great part of four hundred years of caring and contributing and suffering. Theirs was and is the spirit to defeat adversity, with the wisdom and love that helped to make America a better place. These families evolved a vision of a better life and, I hope, a vision of a better South, and a better America.

I believe we all must deepen our understanding of black history. Content is of utmost importance: we need to rectify inaccuracies and distortions. And history must be recorded for broad audiences. Gaps must be closed. The world needs to know of black people's current and past struggles, successes, and contributions. So many people are ignorant about the cultural ingredients that make up multicultural America. Sometimes we are strangers in our own homeland. We must give all readers of all backgrounds a fresh vision of who makes up America's population. So I hope books such as this one can help students learn about this country's diversity.

A seminal moment in American history began with a piece of black history: the death of Crispus Attucks in the Boston Massacre during the American Revolution made this black man the first of America's 600,000 war dead. And continued when a son of one of the people depicted in this book saved the life of the first American enlisted man injured in the Vietnam War. (That Vietnam hero was me, the grandson of freed slaves.)

Dr. Daniel Hale Williams made black history, if not world history, when he performed the first successful open-heart surgery. Edward M. Bauchet made history when Yale made ·him the first black in America to be awarded the doctorate. James B. Parsons went into the history books as the first black federal judge in the continental United States. Charlotte Ray joined black history when she became America's first black lawyer. C. L. Walker, when she became the first American millionaire black woman. The families of John Perry Archer, Nick Archer, Sr., and Chalmers Archer, Sr., made American history when they went from being Mississippi renters to landowners during the Depression years.

This book is intended to seize a truth—a truth that sings, a truth that hurts, and a truth that shatters lies. It is about a people who did not give up on their town, their state, or their country.

Another intent of this book is for our extended family, the Archer family, to tell our history as it happened. The black families of the Delta deserve a special place in history. Those black families had great expectations for themselves and for others. And they did leave their marks on the world!

The core material for this book was written over many years, a bit at a time, reporting events that took place in the lives of us Archer children, to be shared with family and friends, and just for my own enjoyment. There was no thought of publishing these episodes in book form at the time. A most important fact to note is that each experience is expected to stand on its own within each chapter of the book. Sort of as poems or snapshots in the story of life.

Because this is a family history, most of it is oral history, a compilation of many conversations and shared memories. And, like many conversations, it may be rambling and repetitious at times. However, as in all good family talks, you detect patterns of truth, and stir up shared family memories of your own. Also, unlike schoolbook history, this volume has no footnotes; the documentation is mostly the shared body of common knowledge of those who lived in this particular time and place. Oral history may contain errors as well as truth, but I have told this story with a careful attention to the facts. Any errors are mine, and I apologize for them. In the Acknowledgments section that follows, you will find the names of persons, libraries, universities, and other organizations that helped me in my task, and that verified many facets of this story of growing up black in Mississippi.

Acknowledgments

The helpful curators, librarians, and research personnel at the following Mississippi institutions and organizations merit my warm thanks and deep appreciation: Mississippi Department of Archives and History, Archives and Library Division, Jackson; The Mississippi Agriculture and Forestry Museum/National Agricultural Aviation Museum, Jackson; Florcwood River Plantation, Greenwood; The Fannie Booker Museum, Lexington; Trace Park, Belden; The Lexington *Advertiser* Archives, Lexington; The Jackson *Advocate* Archives, Jackson; The Eudora Welty Public Library, Jackson; Lexington Public Library, Lexington; Willie Ellis Center, Lexington; and Smith Roberson Black Cultural Center, Jackson.

In addition to the above resources in Mississippi, the following have provided invaluable assistance: United States Department of Commerce, Bureau of the Census and Library, Washington, D.C.; Library of Congress, Washington, D.C.; Northern Virginia Community College Library, Alexandria Campus, Alexandria, Va.; Fairfax County Public Library System, Annandale, Va.; Afro-American Research Center, Founders Library, Howard University, Washington, D.C.; The Anacostia Neighborhood Museum, Smithsonian Institution, Washington, D.C.; Carter G. Woodson Center, Washington, D.C.; Frederick Douglass Memorial and Historical Association, Washington, D.C.; Moorland-Spingarn Research Center, Howard University, Washington, D.C.; The George Washington Carver Museum, Tuskegee University, Tuskegee, Ala.; and The Hollis Burke Furke Library, Tuskegee University, Tuskegee, Ala.

This book would not have been possible without the skill and the direction provided by my brother A. J. Finch Archer.

He is our family historian, and was the guiding force in all of our efforts. My sisters and brothers—Vernon, Evelyn, Francis, and Hermione—are a tireless, boundless, and dedicated bunch who used their skills, intelligence, and combined efforts to make this project a success. I am grateful to them all, and to my cousins: Nick, Jean, Mary Ann, and Rezell Archer, Ethel Speed, Dottie and Tonja Taylor, Janet and Louretha Land, and Cynthia Boyd. My aunts Esther, Dixie, and Rebecca, and late aunt Edna provided pictures and family records when our fallible memories needed verification of past events. They contributed stories, recollections, and general aid. I cannot do justice to their contributions.

To complete this book required not only the continued support of family but also the support of our colleagues and friends, our "other family" who were part of the project from the very beginning. I want especially to mention Uyen T. Thai, Sophanaren Srun, Chanratana Chet, Sovanny Saray, Lottie R. Kogut, Dianne R. Cogan, Trang T. Mai, Fannie Booker, MacArthur O'Neal of the Holmes County Public Schools, and Mayor Jessie Banks of Tchula, Mississippi.

I am forever indebted to my editor, Mary Kennan Herbert, for her guidance and encouragement. She was always there to offer precise and fruitful suggestions; her counsel and skills were invaluable. I am particularly grateful for her enthusiasm and her sincere belief in the spirit of my story.

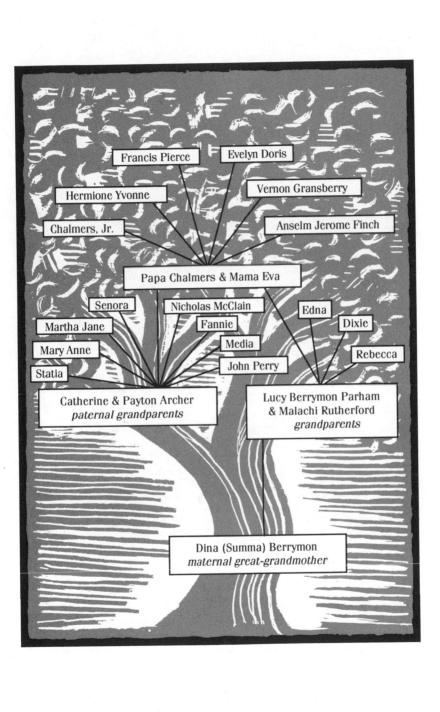

Growing Up Black
in Rural Mississippi

Prologue: Grandpa Payton's Initiation

 When I was eleven or twelve, Papa told me a startling story that Grandpa Payton had told him when *he* was about eleven years old. Grandpa Payton told Papa that, when he was about twelve years old, his "master," the owner of the plantation where he was a slave, had personally taken him into the woods near the slave quarters and, without preamble, whipped him unmercifully. When Grandpa Payton asked why he had been beaten, he was told that he was being taught who was the boss on the plantation and what would happen to him if he did anything the plantation owner disapproved of. End of lesson.

This "rite of passage" evidently made as indelible an imprint on Papa's mind as the actual incident did on Grandpa Payton. Over the years Papa told each of us children about the event with the idea, I guess, of impressing upon us the truly exploitive, amoral nature of slavery.

And, this act of abuse worked. Anyone can readily realize the abhorrent nature of the kind of mind that would calculate the effect such an act would have on a child of eleven or twelve. A child who already found himself in an impossible situation and who must have known that neither parent nor friend could help him. He quickly learned the rules of survival.

Grandpa Payton did not know if this practice was a common occurrence on other plantations in the area. Papa never said that Grandpa had indicated that it was. But, an act of such diabolical intimidation—common practice or not—would indicate that this probably would have been frequently employed for the effect that it must have had on Grandpa Payton.

Even today I often wonder what difference this beating Grandpa Payton endured for no cause of his own made in his life. And I wonder how many other young lives may have been and may yet be crippled by such actions.

It was an initiation our family will always remember, but one we long to forget.

1 The Place

Some of my earliest recollections are of the Place. The Place was a hilltop of about four hundred acres that my father and several of his brothers rented from a wealthy white Tchula family. But whereas Tchula was in the Delta, the Place, though only about a few miles away, was in the hill country. Today, there are no known descendants of the Tchula family from whom we were renting. The Place is now owned by a nonnative Mississippian who seemingly does not use the greater part of the land for any specific purpose. But during the twenty years or so that my father and his siblings lived on the Place, it was a veritable beehive of agricultural activity.

Not long ago my brother and I went back there for a visit; we wanted to pay homage to the Place. However, even though I spent my first twelve years there, I could find no specific, tangible evidence that any of us had ever been there until we found several deeply rutted old wagon paths. Now almost invisible, those paths should have led to where our house once stood. There had been a wagon road leading to other houses too, the homes of kinfolk and many Archers. But the road was gone, the house gone. It was indeed disconcerting to find no evidence of a time that I vividly remember, but, even so, the visit reinforced my memories of the Place and numerous relatives, all gone. Relatives who included Aunt Statia, my father's sister, Uncle Nick and

Uncle Perry, my father's brothers, Bro' John Davis, cousins Ellis and Bunny Baymon.

Look around, and see the memories.

There once stood the house of my father's second-oldest sister, Aunt Statia, and her family. Aunt Statia's husband, Cal Benjamin, was always called Mr. Cal, even by my aunt. Their house was typical of many homes of that era. It was a "dog trot" house that consisted of two sides split down the middle by an open hall where dogs of the family often ran through and slept. Mr. Cal at one time was the owner of the general store and ran the United States Post Office in the area.

Over there was the house where Uncle Nick and his family lived. During his later years when I knew him, Nick Archer was a forceful individual for whom all of us kids jumped when he spoke. He was slightly above average height, thick chested, grizzled, with an always neatly trimmed but bushy mustache.

To us kids, Uncle Nick could do just about anything. He had a blacksmith shop at the Place which was a constant fascination for us. The shop, as it was called by everyone on the Place, was a rather large building near his barn. It had only a dirt floor, but it contained an anvil, drill press, emery wheel, and other tools. These tools were used to repair the farm machinery and other equipment used on the farm and often to make specialized tools that he thought or knew he or others would need. Horses and mules were shod there, and our plow points, hoes, knives, and other tools were sharpened in his shop.

Uncle Nick would move his wood-burning heater into the building during the cold winter months, usually from January to the beginning of spring plowing. He would tinker with his machinery, tuning it for spring and painting away rust. We would help him to sharpen and oil hoes, scythes, and other weeding tools. These tasks were a delight to us as small kids. Uncle Nick's shop was our favorite destination on winter afternoons.

Uncle Nick kept the largest potato hack and smokehouse on the Place. A potato hack is a mound of dirt, corn shucks, hay, and anything else handy that is piled on top of sweet potatoes during winter to protect this highly perishable crop for winter use. The smokehouse is just what the name implies. In this building meats from hog killing were smoked with various woods, including hickory, to cure and preserve them. Of course, in this rural area there was no cold storage, so this activity was of particular importance and Uncle Nick was a master at it. And his orchard at the Place rivaled any in that part of the state; it too is gone.

Uncle Nick had a strong sense of obligation. His family, as did most families on the Place, never borrowed and faithfully paid all bills on time. This policy was scrupulously adhered to so that creditors (whites) could be kept at a distance. Keeping whites at bay was desirable because this was a time and place of racial "rules" that were enforced by intimidating blacks physically, mentally, or through any other means.

Only once did a white man enter Uncle Nick's home with a disrespectful attitude. This was a doctor and former high-ranking official from Tchula. He pushed his way into the house and carried himself in a disapproving manner, a message that black people could not mistake. The doctor was really trying to reach someone who lived on a neighboring plantation; he had gotten lost. Although it was a danger- ous thing to do at that time, Uncle Nick let the doctor know exactly how he felt about his comportment; the gentleman never returned.

Uncle Perry (John Perry Archer) was an easygoing man whose presence was felt everywhere on the Place. I later learned that he was revered because of his devotion to making everyone, including those on the Place who were not Archers by birth, feel as if they were part of the family. Uncle Perry was the oldest brother and had survived the trials and tribulations of his generation of blacks, born so close to the end of slavery.

Uncle Perry had a curious elegance. He was a fair-complexioned man with a ready grin on his face. He was soft-spoken, over six feet tall with a graceful, lean build that complemented his height. He kept his light brown hair closely cut and was always clean shaven.

Uncle Perry had lost his first wife, Miss Rosie, some years before I was born. Miss Rosie was the sister of Bro' John Davis, another tenant on the farm. When Uncle Perry took Aunt Esther as his second wife, he was a school-trained Baptist minister and had a small congregation that he had organized. It was Uncle Perry who officiated at the wedding of my mother and father.

As a man of the cloth, Uncle Perry extended himself to help others. But it was also his nature to do so. He was a mediator and seemed to possess an innate talent to assuage fears, suspicions, and quarreling among those people who lived on the Place.

My most vivid memories of Uncle Perry are associated with the cars he drove. Especially the Model T and the Model As he owned. For most of us, the first time we saw the Model T, it certainly was a strange contraption. We were kind of used to cars by the time he owned the Model As.

Of course, each of the cars scared people and animals alike during Uncle Perry's short drives through the Place. When he drove down the deeply rutted roads after rains, his vehicle was really a sight to see and the noise was something else. His cars were known to frighten all the local horses and mules as they pulled wagons and buggies or plows. Chicken and other fowl were not used to the fast pace of cars and were inevitably killed as opposed to just frightened. Many dogs were killed, too, because they misjudged the speed of the automobile. This was about the only thing we knew of that rubbed people the wrong way about Uncle Perry.

Uncle Perry's house was the "big house." From the time of slavery, it was a gracious, meticulously kept home. When we thought of Uncle Perry's home, we thought of the fig trees in his orchard and that special fig tree at the west end of his backyard. This tree's figs were larger and more delicious than most. We thought of the honeysuckle, the crape myrtles, and the pines around the house. Then far back—past the blossoming orange plants, budding blueberry, and flowering aloe— stood a lone eight-foot mulberry tree full of inch-long mature berries in season. The berries were always delicious. But anyway, fruit picked from Uncle Perry's garden or yard tasted so much better than other fruit.

I remember, too, that outside Uncle Perry's home you could sniff honeysuckles in bloom or hear the mockingbirds sing their hearts out. And if the weather was right, you could catch a sunset while you ate peaches and many other delicious fruit from the orchard. It was the "boss's" home. The eldest son's home. Alas, his big house burned in the middle 1930s.

I often think back on Miss Esther's cooking. She made all kinds of foods, but the desserts stood out.

There were always the "Debby Pies." Delicious Debby Pies. She cooked buttery, brown-sugared apple crisps, and there were the complex, earthy black people's bread pudding, and rich banana cream pie, whose focus was banana, not cream. And the simple, satisfying chocolate pie. For the Christmas holiday, Miss Esther always cooked delightful strawberry pies, topped with fresh-tasting berries and supported by sweet, creamy cheese. The goodies were shared by all who lived on the farm. And visitors were always welcome to try them.

Uncle Perry's way made everyone feel good about themselves. It was said that if you were "touched" by him, you would never be the same again. He and Miss Esther were excellent examples of the so-called Black Puritans of the day. Uncle Perry was a kind man, strongly grounded in his religious convictions. By heritage, industry, and some frugality, Uncle Perry became the landlord and leader for the Archer clan and kinfolk. He was dearly loved by me and by all who knew him. Even so, he was a hell of a driver, and the image of his Ford flashing past our house is a delightful memory. Those cars of his! They enabled him to combine piety with panache.

My brother, who is younger than I, had never seen the Place before. He was perplexed by what we found or what we did not find. There was a dense tangle of trees and an almost impenetrable undergrowth of vines and briars that seemed as if they had always been there. It was hard even for me to believe the overgrown scene spreading before us. All that was left of the old entrance to the Place was a cleared driveway leading to the only house there now, built by the new owner, which occupied one small open niche. Much of the area had been completely overrun by the fast-growing noxious kudzu vine, imported into this country from China and Japan to prevent soil erosion on hillsides. Nevertheless, the opposite proved to be true. The roots of this vine expand and contract in warm and cool weather, letting air and water into the soil and thereby causing the soil to crumble and erode. Erosion caused by this vine is prominent in many areas. Kudzu was planted all over this area of Mississippi by the Civilian Conservation Corps (CCC) during the late 1930s. The overall change in the landscape was astounding.

The boundaries of the Place were almost unrecognizable. One side of the Place had been bordered by an infamous plantation. As my brother and I paced off the lost acreage of my memories, we looked in the direction of the plantation, and I could again hear the bell, I could see a baby covered with flies, I could see a dying cow in agony. Life on that neighboring piece of land was a microcosm of the worst aspects of black life throughout the Deep South. I remember the shanties that were the opposite of the owner's big house. Shanties that had no amenities necessary for civilized life even in those days. Those shanties had dirt floors and sometimes beds that consisted of ticking filled with corn shucks or unginned cotton. I remember Uncle Perry's house and Uncle Nick's house and those shanties, all part of my first twelve years.

Over at the Place, we could always hear the plantation bell that called the tenants to work soon after dawn. This bell also announced when it was time to start and stop the forty-five-minute lunch break, and when it was time to leave the field, at dusk.

On the plantation everybody was expected to do field work except the very old and very young. Even the women were expected to do field work. Many times the older women had to work in the field, then leave and prepare a noon meal, take the meal back to the field for the other workers, then continue field work in the afternoon till dusk. Life on this plantation was as harsh in the 1930s as it had been in the century before.

Health conditions on the plantation were abysmal. Our family often talked about one baby we had observed there. The baby had been left alone for hours because no one was free to care for him. The rest of his family had been required to work in the fields. The baby, completely covered with flies and biting insects, was crying pitifully when we saw him. We always thought it was a miracle that baby survived, but he did.

As was typical on many plantations of that era, tenants were not allowed any land for gardens or to raise livestock. Often a pigsty had to take the place of a yard, or even a room, just to provide meat for the family. Many times the situation for these tenant families became so desperate that some of them took unbelievable action to feed their families. In one instance, the tenants from the plantation stole a cow from the Place, cut out part of the cow's rear hip, and left the animal alive but hobbling—in shock—on three legs. This cow, of course, had to be humanely destroyed.

Despite these grim images, I always seem to think of growing up on the Place near Tchula as one humdinger of a life. As a carefree kid of eight or nine, I had none of the problems of grown-ups, racial, economic, or otherwise. School and chores took up most of the daylight hours, but I remember well the small amount of playtime I had.

My favorite playmate was my cousin and best friend Rezell, who is about two years older than I. Vern, a second cousin, usually played with us. Play was a mixture of imagination and ingenuity. We had this great straw-covered hillside where our barrel staves would carry us flying to the edge of the little gully at the foot of the hill close to Rezell's dad's (and my uncle Nick's) spring.

We also had a perfect sliding place on a high slick clay bank close to cousin Ellis's house. It was worn down to perfection. Sometime in the early evening hours we would lie up there on the bank with a june bug tied to a string and chew sugarcane for long periods. The juice from sugarcane was sweet as the sugar that was made from it and delicious to grown-ups as well as kids. June bugs were a special creature. They were rather large hardbacked beetles that lived on the manure of cattle and horses. Nonetheless, we would catch them, tie strings to their hind legs, and let them attempt to fly away while pretending that they were mail planes that regularly flew overhead. Today, these beetles are often bought by large farmers to rid their pastures of excess manure.

I wasn't aware then, as kids usually never are, of the hard times people were having during the Depression. None of us kids were aware, either, of how hard the work on the farm really was or that all of us were teetering on the brink of economic disaster most of the time.

Although my father was aware of his financial straits, like many men who have fallen in love with cars, he bought a big new Buick. That car was something. It was jet black, sleek, and beautiful—but didn't last too long. Uncle Perry soon wrecked it. Even so, it remained under a shed near the big pond at the main barn for several years. All of us kids would sit in it and pretend we were driving to Lexington, Greenwood, Jackson, Chicago, New York, and around the world.

Papa often told us stories about the old Buick and what it could do. He told about the steep, often muddy hill that led up to the Place; how he would put the car in low gear and let the eight-cylinder engine whiningly claw its way up from the main road. He would then "goose" it on up to the house about half a mile away. That was the last and only car we had for a long time.

I remember the time Papa traded his fine horse Little Mare (who was mine for a time) for a team of mules, Old Tom and Jane. Old Tom was fine and we kids sometimes rode him while Papa plowed, but Jane proved to be dangerously nervous and could not be ridden or trusted. Often a two-animal team was needed for many jobs including plowing, and Papa had to borrow a mule from one of his brothers or a neighbor. So, Jane had to be replaced by Mr. Mack.

Mr. Mack turned out to be lazy, slow, and sneaky mean. Papa once said, "That mule could turn a rank amateur into a certified curser in one morning." Mr. Mack in turn was replaced by Jet, a black mule with white stockings (white coloring on his legs). Jet was adequate at best, while Old Tom became legendary for his smartness and efficiency.

Papa always said that at the time he smoked like a chimney, a habit Old Tom actually made feasible. In those days most people smoked cigarettes that they rolled themselves, and it was hard to roll and smoke while plowing. Papa would roll cigarettes while turning at the end of one row to start down another. This was made easier because Old Tom knew how to pace himself during the turn so Papa could roll and light his cigarettes. If Papa failed to finish the cigarette maneuver before the turn was complete, the mule knew to stop until he finished and then start again. In many ways, Old Tom was probably of more value than the Buick ever was. Mules and horses were essential in those days for cultivating the all important cotton crop and carrying it to the gin. And Old Tom had style.

Papa let me do some harmless center-furrowing of the corn with Old Tom one summer. I also ran the corn planter with Old Tom when I was eight or nine years old. Getting to plow with a mule was a sure sign of maturity. Pretty soon, however, it was back to hoeing, clipping, picking, and doing the chores that came around on a regular basis. Slopping the hogs, feeding the rest of the farm animals, drawing water, cutting and bringing in stove wood—these were the usual chores for nine-year-old boys.

My sister Hermione started pestering Mama to let her try her hand at milking our cow. This soon became one of the great mistakes of her young life. Mama finally said yes, and she more or less got the milking task mastered. But the forbidden pleasure became a chore she despised over all the others. We all had some chores that we hated more than others. Hatred of certain chores did little to get us kids out of doing them, though. We had to earn our keep, as grown-ups were wont to admonish; farming is a family affair.

I remember the late summers with the boiling-hot sun and the dusty crop-laden fields; the pulling of the heavy cotton sacks through the tall cotton stalks. Stooping among the rows to reach the open bolls was a backbreaker even for the smaller kids. And being scratched by black-berry vines and nettles that escaped the choppers' hoes and stung by the stinging worms that my aunt Mama Jane often complained about in later years made for a hard day's work. But it was worth it.

As kids, we loaded many bales of cotton by hand. Loading cotton for the trip to the gin was fun. Cotton was stored at the Place at what turned out to be the most inaccessible spots, in cotton houses or barns, until a bale or one thousand pounds was handpicked. This could take quite a while if only a few individuals were working. The bale of cotton then had to be packed in a wagon with special high sides, using handmade cotton baskets—cotton basket by cotton basket—for the trip to the gin in Tchula. These large cotton baskets were made from strips of oak that were hand split. Similar baskets are still seen in craft shops everywhere.

The ride to the gin was great fun, but the money from the sale of the cotton seeds was more important to us kids. Money from the sale of the cotton was always husbanded closely, for our very future depended upon it. But the small amount of money received from the sale of the seeds themselves was used to splurge on small treats for us kids and the rest of the family. We could expect candy, oil sausages, and other store-bought goodies to supplement our usual fare.

It was a fact of life that our place in the 1920s and 1930s was a complete community unto itself. We really did not depend on the outside world for anything. For us, self-sufficiency was the order of the day for everything but education.

But life as we knew it on the Place came to a halt when our landlord sold the property. He was in failing health, and so the land came under the heavy hand of another wealthy man who was considerably more antiblack than the original owner. We can vividly remember the new owner's first visit to the Place. Papa and his brothers were overheard by us kids as they assessed the situation and pondered what to do.

Papa made his decision after the new owner came to our home for the first time. It was a confrontation not about rent, but about Mama. Papa and others were doing field work, and the owner told him that Mama, a schoolteacher, should also be working in the field. Papa had always said that Mama should take care of the house when not teaching and that he and the kids would do the farm work. He had nightmarish memories of his own mother toiling in the southern heat of summer in the fields. He was very proud of the fact that he had stopped her from doing field work as soon as he was old enough to do so. Papa was outraged to think that this man to whom he was paying rent might also decide who should work in the fields. Within the year all of the families had left the Place.

My brother and I gazed at the spot where our house used to be. We looked down at the remains of the wagon path. We felt the summer heat of long ago, and the presence of Papa as he made his decision to leave.

2 Moving On

My father rented a house for us in Lexington after he decided to leave the Place near Tchula. The house was about two miles from the town on a dirt and gravel road and sat atop a small hill. I suppose that even in 1940 the scene appeared as if it should have been from a time period of even fifty years earlier. The farmhouse had a view of the Balance Due community and a few other houses surrounding this area. The fields appeared to stretch beyond the community without end.

The Balance Due community sits about one-half mile from the town of Lexington. It got its name from a few black families who, after they bought the property from a prosperous white farmer, found that whenever they thought they had finished paying for the property, there was always a balance due. This went on for so long everyone said that they paid for the land ten times over.

Most homes of blacks of that day had a clean space, carefully swept, at the back door. This space served as the playground for the family's children because there was no such thing as school or community playgrounds for blacks. Only one private black school had anything that resembled a sports or recreational area for its students. So the "clean space" at home was the playground. The clean space is thought to have given rise to the derisive ditty of whites, "Where Negroes go, grass won't grow."

Nevertheless, this clean space was the scene of happy times for black boys and girls during this period. Many a fierce game of marbles was played in these spaces. Games that would rival any professional basketball or football game in intensity. Marble games where players favored special shooters as avidly as professional golfers treasure their special clubs—only in these games, players tried to win their opponent's coveted marbles. Black girls played jump rope—especially "double dutch" jump rope, where two ropes are used instead of one—and games like hopscotch because they could draw the grid in the dirt with a stick. When I remember Lexington, I remember hopscotch and marbles, but my boyhood there also is marked by the "grass won't grow" slur.

The house was by no means a grand home, but was acceptable to all of us because of its size and good condition. Nonetheless, we all missed the Place in Tchula a lot. Uncles Nick and Perry and their families also found homes in the same area, but Aunt Statia and her family left the South to live in Chicago. They were fed up with the South; they joined the great migration.

The land around the new house was more hilly and much less fertile than that of the Place, which seriously affected crop production. Papa and Uncle Nick almost immediately came to the conclusion that they would have to find and buy farms with good fertile land. Papa stayed awake many nights trying to puzzle out some means of accomplishing this seemingly impossible feat.

Papa finally noticed in a newspaper a small announcement that the federal government was instituting a program through the Farm Security Administration (FSA). This agency was a forerunner of today's Farm Home Administration and would finance farms for people who met certain requirements, without regard to race. After investigating fully, he found that he and Uncle Nick met the requirements set forth by the FSA.

Though strong resistance was exerted by local officials to keep blacks out of the program, Papa and Uncle Nick were accepted in the FSA program. The federal government, through this program, would provide a home (a new one if the one on the land was inadequate) and land amounts according to family size and other needs. We were soon to have a farm of our own a quarter mile from where we were then living. The farm that Uncle Nick bought was adjacent to it.

Excitement abounded. But upon visiting the new farm site, Mama was greatly disappointed. She described the new home as deplorable. "First, large trees were growing so that their tops met across the top of the road and one seemed to be walking through a tunnel. When we reached the farm a man who seemed older than anyone I had ever seen was sitting on the porch of an old rotting house situated only two or three feet from the road. There was one scraggly pecan tree growing by the front steps. Worst of all, several buzzards were roosting contentedly on top of the house. I cried a lot and resisted Papa's taking the farm. But, I finally agreed to move and was quite satisfied after a new house and barn were built."

It was around this time, 1940, that my cousin and best friend Rezell and I became aware enough to really understand what the adults in the family had been talking about for years. This was probably our time of awakening, and we were a bit frightened but proud even at that young age. It was the family's contention, and that of the larger part of the black community, that black people had to begin to take action on their own in the fight for equality. My father usually expressed such sentiments in his conversations with friends.

"Many of our people on plantations around us are starving from not having the right food or even no food at all. They are being forced to suffer through miserable conditions so we must do anything and everything to help them if the next generation is to have any chance to do better than us. We must set the example so that our children can own land again and not be constantly afraid of losing it through no fault of their own. We know that life is short for black people right now. Our people, especially our children, are suffering through a lack of educational and economic opportunities." To some, his exhortations may have sounded like Uncle Perry's sermons, but Papa's words came from the heart. Another preacher would indeed come along in the 1960s to carry the rhetoric, and the belief, to a wider audience.

However, mild talk such as this was dangerous in those days if it got back to whites in the area. Even having liberal reading matter in the home or coming through the U.S. mail could be dangerous.

There were not many newspapers to read in those days, but our family managed to acquire enough to keep abreast of what was going on in the state and world. Through black newspapers like the *Chicago Daily Defender*, the family could read about accomplishments by blacks and then pass the issues on to those in the community. Keeping up with the news sometimes entailed walking five or six miles to listen to election returns, even though voting was impossible for blacks in the South at this time.

Having just given up the land he had rented with his brothers and other family members on the edge of the Delta, and starting out again on his own, on another farm, Papa was feeling both confident and vulnerable. He had given up most of his livestock, a great deal of the equipment that he had shared with others on the Place, and the active if not moral backing of the rest of the family. His situation was especially difficult because the country was just beginning to come out of the Great Depression. Papa often said, "A large part of the family's food came from the farm's fruit trees and available wild game. I even once killed two rabbits with one shot." He always thought this was quite a feat.

Lexington, in the early 1940s, was a separate and unequal place. This was a place where blacks could not even approach the front door of a white person's home without being screamed at or even harmed. Back doors were for blacks. This was a town where there were "colored only" and "white only" signs on the courthouse bathroom doors and where certain restaurants were known to be off limits to blacks even without signs to say so. This was a town where white policemen could shoot blacks in the back and not even fear coming to trial—and be assured of acquittal at the hands of an all-white jury even if brought to trial. Only registered voters here in Lexington were allowed to serve on juries and, as I said, blacks could not vote anywhere in Mississippi during this era. Every known trick in the book was used to keep blacks from voting—from impossible tests to beatings to actual lynchings.

Under these conditions, money was always a matter of grave concern for blacks. Money other than what could be made from regular crop sales was always needed but extremely hard to come by. For younger blacks, making money to supplement the family income or for themselves was even more difficult. Therefore, making ends meet on the farm was terribly hard when income from crop production did not cover rent, food, mortgages, or other essentials.

At times black families let their wives and daughters do maid's work for more well-to-do white families in their areas. Black boys often hired themselves out to do yard work and other such jobs for these white families, but we Archer kids were never, never permitted to do this. In those days, no matter what the age of white children in those families, blacks were required to address them as Mister or Miss, and Papa always said that this act had caused many black youths to develop feelings of inferiority. Thus, these odd jobs were not worth the small amount that we kids might have made.

But money was so desperately needed that many of us found ways to make money that sometimes were even fun. We could peddle! Peddlers in that day and time were the same as peddlers of any era. We sold everything from fresh fruits and vegetables to wood for cooking stoves. Because we always raised much of what we ate, there was always plenty of things to sell. Truck crops like watermelons were also sold on the farm, but peas, beans, corn—especially corn—were taken from place to place and most times sold well.

There was a downside to peddling that had to be overcome in some way. Since blacks were not allowed to come to the front doors of whites, ways had to be devised so as not to have to go to their back doors. The best approach was to ask the kids or anyone found outside, especially the maids and other workers, to ask the homeowner to come to the door. At times, it angered the whites to find a young black peddler had summoned them to the door, but they usually bought something anyway. Who could resist our homegrown bounty?

Because many of my friends peddled, I would have done so even if I had not needed the money. We would make a game of it. We would make bets to see who could outsell the other. We would bet on who could bring the most to sell and sell everything that he had brought to sell that day for the most money. The loser would have to treat the winner. In later years, I have often thought this was unfair, since some of my friends had smaller places to raise their produce and thus had to work harder to raise what they had to sell. It was fun, though, I have to confess. It's one of those Lexington memories that do make me smile.

3 Conversations with Papa

 Papa was born in Holmes County, Mississippi, in a small rural settlement called the Mount Olive community, between the towns of Tchula and Lexington. He was the youngest of the ten children of Payton and Catherine Archer, both of whom were born in slavery. Papa was born only twenty-seven years after slavery and twenty-six years after the birth of the Ku Klux Klan.

He first left the Mount Olive area for his military service in the First World War. Years later, Mama and Papa took us kids back to Mount Olive and the surrounding areas where they had lived and experienced the major events in their lives. And I could readily imagine the conditions as they were twenty-seven years after slavery.

Mount Olive is approximately seven miles from Lexington; for many years, an unimproved road of dirt and gravel provided the only link. Today, I can see Papa, a ten-year-old boy riding a mule, alone, on the road to Lexington. I can envision his startled meeting with an Indian in the woods. I share his amazement at the sight of a cattle drive. Most of all, I can hear him telling me his wonderful and terrifying tales. I hear him speak.

All of Papa's schooling was at the local school held in the one-room Mount Olive Church, which still survives to this day as a church. It was then a small wooden structure heated by a potbellied wood-burning heater. "The students," Papa said, "every winter would often have to go into the nearby woods, find and cut wood, and build a fire to heat the school before classes could begin.

"The same work was shared by all of the older students. Besides math and English, the schoolwork consisted of a lot of rote learning. We learned lots of poetry and other short works by rote, but our overall learning was exceptionally good for its day. Our teacher was Professor Redmond, a brilliant man who was educated at Alcorn College for Negroes—the first college for blacks in Mississippi." I have often thought that rote learning may have been a good thing. Papa could do mathematical computations in his head as fast as most people could with pencil and paper.

This is what my father told me:

"Many times children would be kept out of school to do field work on plantations, causing them to lag far behind in their education. And students who got behind in their school would sometimes become fully grown and still be in the lower grades. They'd be stuck there until they dropped out in frustration." Then Papa would go on, his voice filling with a deep melancholy:

"In our day, corporal punishment was dealt out freely, and it was saddening and maddening to see grown men, and especially grown women, beaten because they could not keep up with their classes after getting too far behind. The men would be given six lashes across the back or bottom with a large cane and the women six lashes across the lap. I think, rather I know, that many black men and women then decided they would never try school again after such brutal treatment. All because they could not keep up with the work of their age level, through no fault of their own.

"It wasn't uncommon for some of the men to spend all of their time down in the woods surrounding the school 'knocking.' Knocking was basically the act of seeing who could absorb the most punishment from being punched on the order of boxing, only more crudely, as no protective equipment was available.

"We all did a lot of crude and stupid things during those days, I guess. But some were much worse than others. One example of stupidity was the kid who placed his finger on the chopping log at the woodpile after school one day. He jokingly told another student he bet he wouldn't cut off his finger. The other kid grabbed the ax and promptly cut his finger off. I think such cruel inanities, of which there were many, probably resulted from the utter frustrations these young men felt due to the overall situation, economic and social, so they would do just anything to stand out. The young man who cut off his friend's finger left for the big city up North soon afterward. It is chilling to think about what 'mischief' he may have engaged in there even in that era.

"Because Mount Olive was such an isolated community at that time, few resources were available to kids who dropped out of school. So they'd get married and start a family. There usually was no money for anything else." Even I remember well how far away Mount Olive was from both the towns of Lexington and Tchula, before the roads were improved and cars were readily available. But even in the age of the automobile, Mount Olive seemed many worlds away. Or in another time.

This is what my father told me:

"The woods were full of things. Plants used for medicinal purposes grew plentifully throughout the hills and bayous of our area. Some could be sold for a goodly profit by the pound in those days. My sister Fannie and I would frequently go into the surrounding woods to search for plants to sell for anything that we could get. One day when we were in the woods for plants we looked up and found ourselves face to face with an American Indian in full tribal regalia. Cherokee, Choctaw, I don't know, but the sight of the man scared us both out of our wits. To this day, even fighting through the First World War, I don't think I have ever been so scared. It took Mama and Papa a long time to quiet us down and explain what we had seen even though we should have known.

"Seeing Indians, I found as I became a little older, was not at all an uncommon phenomenon. There were lots of them in the area and a great deal of intermarriage between Negroes and Indians. Just look around and see how many Indian-looking Negro people are living around here today.

"In those days," Papa would tell me, "there were many strange sights to be seen in the towns as well as in rural areas like Mount Olive." When I would accompany him on trips to town, there would be many yokes of oxen tied to and around the water troughs near the courthouse. Oxen were almost as common as mules.

"I can even remember cattle drives through the countryside led by Old West cowboy-type drovers taking herds of longhorn cattle through the Mount Olive area. When these drives were spotted, runners would fan out all through the neighborhoods to warn local farmers to make sure their cattle were left outdoors in sight. These drovers would purloin any 'stray' cattle they came across. Anybody who was not warned would, in some instances, look for their 'lost' cattle for many days.

"Until this day, I am still not sure to just what market these cattle were being driven. There was no market big enough to absorb the many cattle that would be in some of those drives. The only logical answer is they were being driven to the Mississippi River near Vicksburg and shipped further by water.

"Mount Olive's seven miles from Lexington was a long and dreary distance for us in those days. There were few houses on the way to Lexington or Tchula, and the landscape was woods for what seemed like miles on end. Many times when Mama or Papa would ask my older brother, Perry, to go to town on an errand, he would pass this chore on to me when I was but ten or eleven years old. Perry would put me on top of one of the family mules or horses and tell me what to do. I would have to make a long, lonely ride into town and then would have to deal with the white merchants, whether I had cash to pay or had to get merchandise on credit. Well, the destination was far worse than the ride.

"Dealing with those merchants at that young age was at times unnerving and at other times downright shattering when they did not trust a young black child. But these chores, I later realized, taught me tact and the ability to deal with objectionable people and situations. Time after time I spent the whole trip to Lexington or Tchula dreading the chore, going over and over in my mind what I would say upon arriving at each particular store depending on the personality of the owner or what clerk was on duty. Those long rides gave me ample time to develop a plan of action.

"The trip to and from town was really rugged in any type of bad weather. The road was graveled in places and dirt in others. Heavy rains would often wash away the gravel on long stretches of the road, and people and beasts of burden would have to slog through the muck and mire of Mississippi mud for long stretches. An example of how difficult this trip was is illustrated by an incident involving a family who owned a wagon with noisy iron wheels. The entire family was returning home in the wagon, coming back from Lexington late one day. The family fell asleep two miles out of town, and the mother fell from the wagon. The noise of the iron wheels on the gravel and pebbles drowned out the cries of the woman trying to alert her dozing family to the fact she had been left behind sprawled in the road. The family arrived at home and discovered the missing passenger, whereupon the father was overheard saying to his oldest son, 'Well sir, Brother, we done lost mother.' Five miles or so back on the dusty isolated road, the family found the frightened woman."

I could easily visualize the conditions Papa was describing. I could well remember the mud-slick road from the Place that led to Tchula. In rainy weather, below the hill, there would be flood waters infested with poisonous snakes. In the bottomlands, people's homes were often built on stilts. Even then, water would still rise to their doors and these people would have to get around in boats. During one spring flood I became somewhat of a local hero when I saved my younger cousin, who had fallen from the porch of one of these houses into this murky water.

Like many rural areas in Mississippi during this era, Mount Olive was such an isolated and insular community that intermarriage was not uncommon. "In fact, there was a great deal of intermarriage. Most people in this neck of the woods were related," my father said. "After Eva and I were married I learned that Miss Lucy [Eva's mother] and I had many of the same relatives. Take, for example, the Baymons. As you know, Bill and Bunny and all the rest of them are closely related to both of us. Miss Lucy was a Baymon. It's the same family."

Papa said he could remember reading somewhere that an African runner explained how he and others from his tribe became effective long-distance runners. "The runner said they lived so far from the nearest school they would have to leave home at daybreak and run for several hours to arrive on time for the beginning of classes. I remember the African saying, 'We became so adept at running, as a result, many times we would run down rabbits and other small game and carry dinner home with us.' "

Hunting tales! We kids loved to hear tales of hunting and fishing prowess. Papa would, at times, go on for hours about how, as children, he and his brothers, cousins, and friends would get together in groups and go hunting. Since most of them were too poor to own guns or get ammunition for any they had, they would hunt, like the African athlete, by running down rabbits with sticks.

"We would go out looking for sticks that had a small nodule or rounded lump on one end so that they could be thrown short distances with great accuracy. If none were found, the boys who were good at carving would make one for the rest of us. Some of the boys would become so adroit at throwing their special sticks that we would kill as many as sixteen or seventeen rabbits in one afternoon. I have since always felt an affinity for the life that this African runner lived in his youth, or maybe he would feel an affinity for mine."

Papa said that his stint in the United States Army was not, overall, an auspicious occasion. "I was literally plowing the south forty when I was sent for by the Lexington military draft office and told to report there at once. I was told that I would be summarily jailed for not answering previous notices to report for induction into the army. The only thing that kept me from being jailed was the report from the postmaster who said no letter had come through the post office for Chalmers, as she knew me personally.

"Nevertheless, I was not allowed to even return home and change clothes or tell my parents—Grandma Catherine and Grandpa Payton— where I was and what was happening to me. I was inducted into the army on the spot. We were shipped out by train the next day, and as we passed through southern towns we were called opprobrious names by the whites who had come to see the colored boys off to war. They called us names, even though we were on our way to fight for our country.

"Although our battalion was all black, all of our commanding officers were white. This was true even after we reached Camp Dix in New Jersey. Lesser officers were black, but they had to strictly adhere to orders given by the higher white officers. If a black officer decided his men should have five minutes' rest because of a vigorous training schedule, we would have to go right back to training if a white officer decided we should, no questions asked.

"On the ship going overseas, most of the men became desperately ill from seasickness. Some of the boys died. I think the only thing that saved me was someone told me to eat raw white potatoes and nothing else. The ship would be rocked by one-hundred-foot waves, and many of us, though thoroughly frightened, would find ourselves hanging over the sides, heaving from seasickness.

"When we arrived in France we were divided into two groups. Those of us who could read were put into one group and told what fighting battalion we were to be with, whereas the boys who could not read were put in companies that were made to do the menial chores like digging trenches, graves, and latrines. I lost all contact with these men, the ones who could not read, and never saw most of them again until I returned stateside. They did menial labor for white and black units throughout the war.

"While in France we would walk for miles each day. Like all soldiers, we would carry full gear that seemed to weigh a ton by nightfall. The weather was often so cold I couldn't even feel my feet. Some of the heavier men had terrible feet problems." Papa often told of soldiers whose feet split open during the long walks because of their lack of adequate previous exercise.

"Upon our return to this country, we landed in New York City. Because we had served with distinction during the war, we were given a ticker tape parade, something none of us had ever witnessed before. But because we were an all-black group, our commanding general would not march with us. He publicly stated that he was not going to be seen with a bunch of colored boys.

"Otherwise we were treated decently, at least, upon our return to this country—until we reached our mustering out base in southern Mississippi. There we were held for days without food and made to do meaningless work. We were even made to break rocks as if we had been sentenced to hard labor until we all banded together, sat down, and went on strike.

"Groups of men would collect what money that could be collected, slip off base, and buy food that would be cooked over outdoor fires. We were told by the white officers that they would show us that we were back in Mississippi now and not some goddamn celebrities in a goddamn ticker tape parade in New York.

"It took us two months to 'fight' our way back home from the base in southern Mississippi. There was, I found, no change in the way we lived, upon my return to Mount Olive. The day I came home, my mother was in the field helping my brother Nick. It was then that I decided that she should no longer do any type of field work. Joking, I promised to 'fuss at' her myself if she didn't leave the field right then and if I ever found her in anybody's field again. I was a war hero from France, and that's the only way I could let out my frustrations. That was the one change in our lives I could make. But, as I look back on it now, I soon fell back into the same routine of life from before leaving for the war."

Mama and Papa were married on the Place near Tchula soon after Papa returned from the battlefields of Europe. Papa was somewhat older than Mama when they were introduced to each other by his niece, his sister Statia's daughter, Archie Benjamin, who had instituted a determined matchmaking effort immediately upon Papa's return from the war. His niece was successful. The marriage lasted for more than fifty years.

Both Mama's and Papa's parents were enthusiastic backers of education. They always urged their children to continue their schooling as long as possible. But with the intervention of his service in World War I, and the illness of both parents soon thereafter, Papa did not get the chance to further his education beyond the equivalent of high school. Nevertheless, he worked hard at his chosen profession of farming, which he loved, as scientifically as anyone in the area, black or white. I can remember seeing him poring over such publications as the *Farm*

Journal and the *Progressive Farmer*, as well as government publications. His self-preparation and hard work paid off, for his production was usually higher than anyone we knew of. Essentially, he farmed all year long.

Papa's search for insight into the latest farm methods led him to an avid interest in the Tuskegee Institute in Alabama, now Tuskegee University. George Washington Carver was doing world-renowned research in agriculture at Tuskegee, and Papa followed his work closely, faithfully employing whatever procedures Dr. Carver suggested. Papa once went to hear Booker T. Washington speak in the all-black town of Mound Bayou, Mississippi. Booker T. Washington was the founder and president of Tuskegee. "I never saw so many people gathered to hear one man speak and listen so attentively to what he had to say before," Papa said. "I agreed with most of what Booker T. had to say that day, but disagreed with his philosophy of casting down one's bucket wherever one was. This smacked of the white man's idea that black people should be satisfied with what they had, rather than make any attempt to better themselves.

"Booker T. Washington had long been known to hobnob with influential whites, even, it is said, to ride in the whites-only section of the segregated trains, but thought other blacks should not. Thus, statements like 'cast down your bucket where you are' were not favorably received by many. However, his school was first-rate and he was impressive overall." I think this trip by Papa was the prime reason I was sent to Tuskegee Institute many years later, and I still think of Tuskegee as *the* school.

This is what my father told me:

"During the winter when the weather was too bad for any farm work, my brother Perry, some friends, and I would go into the woods for logging. This was hard, dangerous work but we did it day after day to supplement our incomes.

"There were no power saws or power lifts to handle the large trees that had to be felled and brought out of dense forests by specially trained horse and mule teams. These trees had to be felled by two-man cross-cut saws and axes and brought to whatever roads available by large and spirited teams of animals, even yokes of oxen. Many people ended up with broken bones and were even killed doing this tough, tricky work.

"We would use some of this lumber to produce roofing shingles. Using only cross-cut saws, chisels, mauls, and axes, we would produce stacks of cedar and oak shingles along with cedar posts. They would then be hauled the ten miles from Tchula to Lexington by wagon. Many of these shingles and cedar posts have been spotted on local farms today. I still have a couple of the cedar posts that Mr. Cal and I hauled to Lexington in 1932. Those cedar posts seem to last forever."

Before Papa started farming again around 1923, he worked four or five years at what he always referred to as public work. He said he worked at an icehouse that was the first in Holmes County. He described how large blocks of five hundred pounds of ice were made and loaded onto trains at the switching station in Gwin, Mississippi, near Tchula. Papa said working inside the icehouse was miserably cold and handling the ice under those conditions was numbing.

To make clear ice for home use, the ice was started from hot water that was cooled as rapidly as possible. This ice was usually sawed into twenty-five- or fifty-pound blocks and sold to commercial icehouses for resale at retail markets. Retail icehouses would store the ice either in sawdust or under burlap and sometimes peddled it from house to house by horse and buggy. "Everybody, especially field hands, were glad to see the ice man coming in hot weather," Papa said.

Papa also said that at one time during his tenure of public work he also did every job possible in railroad work. "I have laid track in hundred degree weather day in and day out," Papa often said. "But the most illuminating and worst railroad job that I held was 'call boy.' In this job I had to awaken various workers in time to report for their jobs. All of these jobs were held by white workers and when I would awaken them at two o'clock in the morning, they would call me every name I had ever heard. Some would even throw their shoes or other objects at me with all the strength they could muster. It was after the repeated experience of being called boy, and worse, as a 'call boy' that I decided that railroad work was not for me."

Another tale would come to a close. A pause. And Papa would shake his head and say, "Oh, I have *worked* in my life." He worked up to the day he died, just short of his ninety-sixth birthday.

4 Uncle Nick

There is just one photo of Uncle Nick as a young man that the family knows of. The picture was a big one, and to me and the other kids, it was larger than life. The portrait was of him and five or six of his friends. It was an old picture but was of good quality, and hung in the inside hall of his home in Lexington.

When I looked at Uncle Nick in the photo with his friends, I could see he was a strong young man who stood about six feet tall and weighed around 185 pounds. He was also about half a head above his companions in the picture and appeared to outweigh them by fifteen to twenty pounds. At that young age he had a somewhat oval face and closely cropped hair. He didn't have a mustache then. The overalls he wore were typical for farm life in that era.

One could sense that he was a simple young man, like the rest of the men in the picture, with no visible badge of acclaim. He would not, at first glance, seem to merit any special recognition. Yet, as he stood there looking out from the old frame, to me he seemed a giant. Something about his photograph said he understood his own abilities. He projected the image of a young person who knew who he was.

Now this is what the other kids in the neighborhood and I were told about Uncle Nick and his early years. He was strong, he was fit, but not extraordinarily muscled. Nevertheless, he could out-climb, outrun, and out-fight most of his peers. We were also told that he was personable and compelling without being especially handsome. He was reserved in manner. We were told that he did not greet even his few close friends heartily, for he was somewhat reserved about greetings altogether. Yet everyone said that he had a tremendous drive. And that he was very, very respectful to his elders and was always willing to give a helping hand to anyone in need. This meant all people, not just black people.

Our family still tells many special stories about Uncle Nick when he was growing up. Papa especially liked to talk about how Nick looked out for and protected him, his youngest brother; he said that Nick was not scared of anything and would try anything twice.

Early on, it became a known fact in our family that one of the times Uncle Nick misbehaved as a youngster was when he slipped away and went boating on mysterious Tchula Lake. This was a place the family were never, never to go. There was an unwritten law against boating and fishing on the lake that applied only to black people—under the threat of death. Naturally, the lake was irresistible to a young boy.

The family often joked about one particular high jink Uncle Nick perpetrated when he was older. That was the time when (possibly drunk as a skunk) he turned loose a bag of snakes in the Mount Olive Church during a revival meeting. On the night of the snakes incident, Miss Suckie lost her shoes and Miss Kate her apron. "I can hear Mama now," Papa said. "She'd say, 'Nick, you must not give the Archer name a bad reputation, good names are hard to come by. We worked long and hard for our good name, don't drag it in the mud. Our name is worth its weight in gold!' "

The snake episode caused quite an uproar. And out of it all came some mighty fancy tales. How tall the tale was depended on who was telling it. Some people just tried to explain what really happened; others told stories that made people laugh, stories that made some people think, stories that frightened a few people, or even stories that took people's minds off their troubles for a while. One thing for certain, the incident completely drove out the entire congregation from church that night.

One of the tales about that night focused on a small kid who got separated from her parents in the confusion. A big python snake was supposed to have wrapped itself around the child and began to make off with it. When the child started to cry, someone spat in the snake's eyes. The python then let the child go. As soon as that happened, the snake died. After that story, people said that if you spit in a snake's eyes, it will surely die.

Clusters of frightened congregants leaving the church had different reports about what happened. Mr. Will Holmes, a close friend of the family, told this story: "The first group I ran into that night told me that somebody had turned loose over a thousand snakes and crocodiles in the church during the revival meeting, and that two or three grown church members were swallowed whole.

"Another person said, 'First all we could hear were the sounds. Shuffling noises, as if someone was dragging a peg leg across the floor. Ssht, ssht, sshhhtt. . . . Then we saw some of the serpents speed-sliding across the church floor. Some were spitting poison at us. Then all we could hear were screams.' 'If only we had had some sulfur or mothballs, we would have been protected,' another added.

"They also told me that a crocodile bit an arm of a church member. The lady, they said, managed to drag herself up to the low fence outside of the church and fall over to the other side. She nearly bled to death. This group told me that the only reason they were still alive was because they 'lived the gospel.'

"Some church members in another bunch I met claimed there were at least two boa constrictors running around loose in the church and the big snakes were writhing around all over the place. And that the snakes swallowed two children whole."

In Tchula's white households, the stories went something like this: Someone turned loose a big python snake out at the black folks' Mount Olive Church the other night. Aunt Matilda tells us that the snake poked his head up between two benches and rose up like a man, sticking out his tongue and looking all around. The reason the snake was even there, they said, was because the congregation had those pots turned down in the middle of the floor to keep us white folks from hearing what they talked about. (During slavery time, pots were turned down to "capture" voices, preventing them from being heard at distances.)

There were also many stories about the episode from other sources. But in fact, Uncle Nick told us, the "snakes" he released were shiny lizards, "slow-worms," garter and glass snakes, and black snakes. None were poisonous. A kitten could harm more people than a very alarmed nonvenomous snake, he said. In any event, according to Uncle Nick, the poor creatures were simply trying to escape the pandemonium caused by the worshipers.

Young Uncle Nick would sometimes go to a lot of trouble to make his antics "successful." Especially when the shenanigan had a serious intent. One stunt was deadly serious with a purpose that made it dangerous for him and his partner in crime. This partner was Ira Thomas, a close friend who was also a distant cousin. The purpose of the stunt was to offset the effects of the Ku Klux Klan, using hard-earned knowledge about the KKK's organization; to ridicule and bring into the open the cowardice of the Klan; and to spread the word into the Mount Olive community that Klan members (usually called white-cappers) were ordinary humans and not ghosts.

But first, in working out his plan, Uncle Nick had to further promote the ghost story before he could pull off the stunt that would be performed at the site of a "haunted bridge" and near a "hanging tree." The bridge was east of Tchula, about two miles out on Sheno Road.

This was a ghost tale in which Uncle Nick could really exalt. Actually, the story had been around for a very long time, and some said it had been told by black families since slavery time. Of course, with Uncle Nick's help, the story became centered on his home town of Tchula. And the neighboring communities buzzed anew with tales of the bridge and tree. The family later learned that our uncle's involvement was well thought out and planned.

The ghost tale about Gwin Creek Bridge and a lone hanging tree went something like this: During early Reconstruction, the Klan took a number of black people to the bridge and lynched them. The victims' hands were tied behind their backs and they were forced to sit with their feet hanging over the side of the bridge. As they sat on the bridge, the Klan shot them like rabbits, one at a time, with the victims falling from the bridge's edge into the water. The bodies lay where they fell for days with the threat of death to anyone who moved them.

The hanging tree was, and still is, a tall tree that measures about four feet in diameter. Today, the tree is still close to the rebuilt bridge, at the right edge of the creek as one travels east from Tchula. At the opposite side of the bridge is a small branch of the main stream, made up of a number of pools held together in a chain by a series of tiny waterfalls and rapids. The branch stream carved about a twenty-five-foot gully and was bordered by heavy growth. The tree still has the "handy" limb from which a number of people, both black and white, were hanged.

Everybody said that babies cried almost every night under Gwin Creek Bridge. A galloping jet black horse and a deer as big as a grizzly bear were spotted nearby every once in a while. And there were strange footsteps, eerie lights, and unearthly voices. Uncle Nick went to lots of trouble to make the stories a reality. He used his mechanical and artistic know-how to do this.

Uncle Nick built small seaworthy boats about the size of a shoe box to float acetylene lamps down the creek to create eerie floating lights. This was done just before groups of people crossed the bridge and often enough to keep the "hant" story going. He also built the lamps himself. His cousin Ira was always downstream to reclaim the boats and lamps. For sound effects, the two used an old violin, blew through cigarette paper placed across a comb, blew a flute, and played a mouth harp. In the far background were always howling dogs and sometimes screaming cats. All of this was leading up to something big.

Our aunt Mama Jane, the eldest sister, told this story. "My brother Nick used painted, inflated animal bladders to make frightful, grinning ghosts and other spooky spirits with pasted-on arms, or in some way made the pig bladders look like little men with outstretched arms. He sometimes weighted the figures' bases with sand or water and floated and whirled them across the creek on ropes and pulleys. These figures appeared to be suspended in a blaze of crimson light, while they seemed to alternately beckon and flitter in anguish. We never found out how Nick produced the weird phosphorescentlike glows. Some said that he used petrified wood and others said that he used some type of lamps that he had made. Nick simply would not tell us."

We do know that Uncle Nick built a skeleton with a carved head, which grinned in a way that only a skull can grin. He then outfitted it in a white bush shirt and trousers rotted to tatters and sat it at a table in the middle of the running creek. The skeleton was with a family scene of husband and wife and three children all securely fastened in chairs around a dinner table.

The "family" consisted of coats and trousers filled with straw, and with old shoes attached. The heads attached to the figures were carved from pumpkins and had very small candles mounted inside. The scene included the table with a room of furniture, food, and dishes on the table. A kerosene lamp was on the middle of the table. There were bright curtains and painted sheets for backdrops. Along with all of this were the usual eerie sound effects. These things could be hidden or taken away within a matter of minutes.

Uncle Nick had to know the exact schedule of the Klan's night meetings to carry out his escapade. But this did not prove to be a problem. He had a girlfriend who cooked in the home of a prominent member of the Klan. In addition, his close friend Charles Johnson, a fellow blacksmith, knew the ways of white folks and their news and secrets. Often more than other whites did. Charles Johnson's shop was a popular hangout for all kinds of white people. Besides, the Klan's schedules were common knowledge to some black people. Perhaps even more among black people than among whites.

Tchula's KKK members had to cross the Gwin Creek Bridge and pass the hanging tree to get to their regular meeting site, the Little Red School House, which was about a mile from our home.

Lincoln Polk, a cousin and neighbor in Lexington, at a later time told this story: "It was crisp autumn time. The particular night of the Klan's meeting, Nick and Ira waited for just the right moment, until the group of Klansmen came down the road in their old truck with the tall-sided wooden bed behind the cab. There were so many members in the truck that they had to stand like cotton pickers on their way to the fields. The night was inky black and cold, and the wind moaned low and long.

"There was only muffled talk from the people in the truck as they passed the hiding place of Ira and Uncle Nick. But then they reached the deep curve in the road and began to go down the sharp hill just above the bridge. They must have spotted the 'ghost scene' at the same time. And there were the eerie lights and the unearthly voices made by Uncle Nick and Ira. Anyway, there was total panic. The driver jumped from the cab, abandoning the truck, which ran into a ditch. Tchula's senior police officer was with the group."

No one knows exactly what happened next, but the Klan members left behind their sheets, their hoods, some pistols, knives, and rifles in and near the truck. Most made their way to nearby black cabins screaming that "ghosts are all over!"

None of the Klan were brave enough to return to the bridge until the following morning. Some time later when the police chief, his two assistants, and six other men returned with guns in hand and pistols in their pockets, they found no evidence of ghosts. They did, however, find their overturned truck. Gone were the sheets, hoods, and weapons. The truck was a total loss as a result of its "fall" from the bridge. The word got around in the black communities.

Strangely, even today, there is something weird, and seemingly unnatural, about the bridge and nearby hanging tree. And they both still excite local and regional curiosity because of their haunted reputation.

When Papa kidded Uncle Nick about his antics as a young fellow, he inevitably would come back with, "Chat, you don't know what you're talking about!" But from what we children learned, Uncle Nick may have seemed incorrigible, but didn't have a mean streak in his body. "You really couldn't meet a kinder fellow," Uncle Perry, Uncle Nick's oldest brother, told us one day. On further reflection, he added: "But Nick was quick-tempered enough." Grandma Catherine was known to say, often, "Nick is my cross to bear. My one big burden."

Papa told us about that one boat ride with Uncle Nick on Tchula Lake. "Nick took me once," Papa admitted. "Tchula at that time was largely along, but back from, the shore of the lake. To young folk of that generation, the whole town seemed mostly made up of bayous. Dark water was everywhere."

Papa told us about that ride with Uncle Nick in an unseaworthy canoe that took them slowly past bald cypress and other huge trees in the shallows. They continued about a mile toward the Gwin settlement and then past houses that were built on stilts out over the water. "It was Nick's special place, and was truly beautiful and totally deserted." Papa told me about "the event" one evening as he and I boated down the lake many years later.

On that trip, through a break in the trees and growth, we spotted a very large antebellum home. It was not only wide but tall, and the dependencies attached to the back made it great in length. Papa said that day, "If we were up close during springtime, we would see the kitchen garden fully planted in red tulips. During the autumn months, the red salvi there attracts hummingbirds by the dozens," he said. Papa had visited the house two or three times with his sister Mama Jane.

As Papa told it, "During the daylight hours of the boat ride, there was a cool, gentle, mildly flower-scented breeze drifting toward us, and the image of the sun cast its light through the trees down on us making its own game of shadows. There were the usual swarms of turtles and snakes on the logs and timbers. The rest of the world seemed to disappear. Part of the way the sky was crystalline blue, with gulls gliding overhead and the sun glittering on the water like diamonds. On the return trip, a full moon lit our way. Only in Mississippi were there places so striking."

During those days, Tchula Lake was crystal clear. "Most white people who lived nearby spent considerable time relaxing on or near the water," Papa told us. Black people, too, if accompanied by a white person. There was excellent fishing, plus plenty of space for boating and swimming. Tchula Lake was, and still is, one of Holmes County's most scenic waters.

"At times we glimpsed from our boat cotton fields that were the 'crops of the planters.' There were long straight cotton rows as far as your eyes could see. Very seldom in the Delta did one spot cornfields or sugarcane patches or the like. Plantation owners in the area were interested only in cotton since it was the major cash crop," Papa said.

"Anyway, we could see how the lake was narrowing, and I asked Nick, 'Where does the water go from here if we kept on, instead of turning around and heading back for your secret place? Where would the lake take us?' And you know what he said? He told me that if we continued, 'we would disappear with the lake into the great swamp of hell!' "

But there was also a serious side to Uncle Nick. Although he was not too interested in schooling, he had lots of natural ability. Even as a very young person of sixteen or seventeen years of age, he could do just about anything. He was also very dependable. If there was a job to be done on the farm or anyplace else, he acted responsibly, arriving early in the morning, kicking up swirls of dust with Grandfather Payton's horse and buggy. He would unload his tools and start to work. He would then paint and mend. He fixed bicycles, watches, and motors. He renovated big houses and cottages. He built greenhouses and smokehouses. He could lay a brick walk or build a potato hack.

There seemed to be no job that the world could throw at Uncle Nick that he could not do. Everybody from miles around sooner or later came to him, understanding that what he did was of lasting value.

We were told how Uncle Nick touched things the way sculptors do. Lumber was probably his marble. His fingers roamed the surface, searching . . . what for? Perhaps finding blemishes. Or perhaps it was just his way of approaching the wood as someone might a horse— "settling it down." As he worked, he was, probably even at that tender age, alone with his thoughts or without any at all. This had to be paradise for him.

Aunt Statia, Papa's and Uncle Nick's second-oldest sister, told the story of a shed that Uncle Nick made for the big house where Uncle Perry lived. The shed was for trash boxes. It had three compartments, one for each box, and it opened from the top for putting in trash sacks and from the front so the boxes could be removed. He made it so each lid worked perfectly. He also made it so the lids hinged one way and then another. It looked good.

"But Uncle Nick was not finished," Aunt Statia said. "He painted the little shed gray and let the paint dry. I went out to look at it, amazed that it could be so lovely. I put my finger on the paint and found it dry. The work was done, I thought, but the next day my younger brother Nick was back with sandpaper and to rough up the paint.

Every so often he would feel with his fingers, searching out what he could not see. He was adding another coat, he said, although to my eyes it did not need one, and in truth, could have done without one. That is the way Nick worked, though. He worked to perfection. He was good, really good."

Uncle Nick told me one day, "I tried, in my own way, to use my skills to prove that black people could do things as well as white people. I have learned of other black people who did the same thing, in a big way. People like Elijah McCoy, Benjamin Banneker, Garrett Morgan, and Dr. George Washington Carver, to name just a few."

Other family stories tell about times when Uncle Nick would cook to impress the ladies or just cooked Sunday dinners for Grandma Catherine and the family. It was no place to be if you did not want to get fat. His meal for the women might feature baked ham, biscuits, mashed potatoes, green peas, fig preserves he made himself, and always a three- or four-layer cake of some type.

Aunt Fannie, his younger sister, told us about his family breakfasts: "When we got up in the morning, it was in a house that smelled of breakfast food and we would sit at a smoking table full of fat, juicy bacon or fatback, brains and eggs, ham, hot biscuits, fried apples soaked in Nick's special syrups, honey, fresh butter, fried steaks, hot coffee, and grits. Or there were stacked pancakes, Louisiana molasses, sausages he stuffed himself, bowls of wet cherries, plums, and jam. His specialties for all occasions were hoecakes, okra, peanuts, and black-eyed peas."

Uncle Nick's great cooking secret was his hearthside formulas. That included the fires, the tools, and the techniques. The hearth, which he had built himself, was inside a brick building at Uncle Perry's house. People were stunned by the size of the hearth. To me, as a small boy, it was enormous, with many cranes, pots, and kettles. When he cooked, the utensils were said to be both in and on the fire. His hearthside recipes were mouth watering. Many are lost to the world, but here is one that the family uses to this day:

WALNUT CIDER RICE

¼ *cup chopped onion*	½ *teaspoon salt*
¼ *cup chopped celery*	½ *teaspoon ground cinnamon*
2 *tablespoons butter*	½ *cup chopped walnuts*
1 *cup apple cider*	¼ *cup diced apples*
1 *cup uncooked rice*	

Uncle Nick cooked it this way: using a medium-size pan, he would beat up the onion and celery for about a minute and a half in the butter, over red-hot coals, until crisp and tender. Next, he would add the cider, rice, salt, cinnamon, and a cup of water. The mixture was covered and then brought to a boil over red-hot coals. Cooler coals were then used, but he kept them hot enough to simmer the food for about twenty-five minutes, or until all the water was boiled out. Care was taken to add hot coals as needed. Finally, he'd add the apple and walnuts. The finished dish was covered and placed away from coals to stand for at least five minutes.

Another Uncle Nick story I'll always remember is about the time when he beat up a group of four or five white boys single-handed, and invited them back for more. One of the boys had called him a name. This is the way Uncle Nick was. He fought often with individual white boys his age. But he also fought with black boys too. Nick simply would not take anything from anybody without a fight.

Most of the fights were with white boys who were at Nixon's country store. "The store was a place where races mixed well, considering that it was during the early 1900s," Uncle Nick told me one day. "Black people patronized the store together with whites, often spending only a few cents. This was the day of striped penny candy and five-cent drinks," he said. "I remember that there was more familiarity and friendliness at the store than anywhere else during those times of Jim Crow laws and strict customs that worked so well to separate the black and white races. But invariably, some white boy, usually in the company of five or six of his friends, would approach me with a push or shove or come across with an off-color, racist remark. I would simply proceed to knock his block off. Most of the time I lost the fight because the whole gang jumped me."

Those were the days of drinking from "colored only" and "white only" water taps and of segregated waiting rooms. Of stark racial hatred. Of murders, lynchings, and disappearances of black people, both men and women, throughout Mississippi. Uncle Nick's insistence that he was as "good as the next person, black or white," landed him in the Tchula jail many a Saturday night. This also meant tangles with Tchula's chief of police. Uncle Nick simply wouldn't get off the sidewalk to let white people pass. He invariably was bested by the nightsticks and brass knuckles of the Tchula police. "Those were some of the most painful experiences of my life. Ours was a troubled land in those days," he said.

Young Uncle Nick was better known for his carpentry skills and cooking expertise than his ideas about civil rights. During later years, he frequently let it be known to us younger family members that he never really hated anybody, even the chief of police: "My recollections of those times are not tinged by hatred. It's just that I couldn't understand how some human beings could treat other humans so badly because of their color. I felt so sorry for them. I felt so sorry for them," he would repeat, remembering the folks who had caused so much pain.

5 A Poor Black Farm Kid

 One of my earliest recollections of living on our rented farm, called the Place, near Tchula, Mississippi, was when we two oldest children in our family were about three and four years old. One morning the two of us ventured all alone out the back door of our house and scampered carefree as can be down the path to beckoning freedom. Grasses, taller than toddlers, lined both sides of the path, and hid us from parental scrutiny.

Beautiful trees and cotton fields stretched enticingly in front of us. Hills framed the landscape to the far right and left of us, and we were now running as fast as we could. Everything was soft, and sweet, and pastoral, a garden of Eden for us kids. To us children, the sights around us were simply the most divine in the world.

Suddenly, with a great, great hiss from under a cotton stalk near the path, a fat snake shot across our way. We both saw it at about the same time. Our terror was so general and natural that, in our mutual memories at least, we became all legs and mouth as we ran home to Mama or where we thought the back door was, hoping to leave behind us the grim, fanged road.

That night we two kids both dreamed of large poisonous snakes. Ghostly hostile snakes. Aggressive snakes. One of us dreamed of snakes large enough to swallow children whole. The other dreamed of serpents that stuck their fangs into you and would not let go. For quite a while, both lost trust in our Eden. It was a traumatic experience that marked that summer, the first but certainly not my last encounter with Mississippi snakes.

Life on the farm during the Great Depression probably resembled farm life of fully one thousand years before than it does some farms today. All ten families on the Place, except Uncle Perry's, lived in wood clapboard houses alongside small wagon roads which ran the length of, and across, the Place. The houses always looked neat as a pin, the floors clean enough to eat on.

Although pleasantly cool in the summer, the houses were cold in the winter. Thick wooden shingles on the roofs and wood stoves in the kitchens were of marginal value in warding off the cold. Heat came from fireplaces with two single, sometimes double chimneys. The kitchen stoves—or ranges, as they were sometimes called—often had water warmers attached on the sides. Ours did. Most houses had no heat in the sleeping rooms, but hot bricks and pressing irons and down quilts and covers helped to keep us warm during the cold winter nights.

Single or double outhouses in back sufficed for sanitation. Outhouses were always placed downhill from water supplies. There were cisterns for convenient drinking water. And many types of drinking springs were within walking distance. Water for bathing was heated on wood stoves. Water for washing was heated in a multipurpose pot in the yard, burned black from use.

Some yards were covered with white sand, replaced every spring from nearby sand pits. Others had regular suburban-style lawns that were trimmed with push mowers and swing blades. The sand lawns were kept clean by sweeping once or twice a week with brush brooms.

There were always dogs, chickens, guineas, ducks, and geese in the yards. Families on the Place all raised chickens, and hens and guineas nested in every convenient place: alongside buildings, in the fork of a tree, and wherever else the hens had an inclination to lay. Sometimes even in the chicken house. Finding the nest locations was one of my jobs.

Hog pens were always well away from our living quarters for

sanitation reasons. Hog killing and cattle butchering were a community affair.

The outstanding part of our backyards was the woodpile with large stacks of oak and hickory and pine for burning in the fireplaces and cooking stoves. Chinaberry, mulberry, magnolia, peach, plum, and fig trees gave us shade. We kids also used these trees for treehouses and climbing. All of these things gave us pleasure, and I did not think of myself as a poor black farm kid.

All and all, for both kids and young adults, the Place was a wonderful, relatively comfortable, and happy place to be and live. It was a complete, perfectly ordered world, even with the occasional intrusion of snakes. This was the rural black southern life for some children in the 1930s whose parents at least rented the land, even if they did not own it.

Today, when I look back through the eyes of an adult on those days past, I realize that my earlier perception of the Place and Tchula was wrapped in a mystical haze. I fully realize, now, that it was a time of murders, lynchings, and disappearances. Mississippi was a cornucopia of rich soil, the scent of magnolias, blood, and violence. Those were the days when fears and hatreds haunted a troubled land. It was a time when black people's lives and the lives of their families were always on the line. There was a pervasive feeling among black people that whatever they said or did about anything would make absolutely no difference.

It did not mean as much to me in the 1930s, but I now remember an incident on the road to Tchula, right below where we lived. John Kiles's oldest son was shot in the back with a rifle so powerful that the bullet passed through his body, tore a hole in his chest, and then shattered a front window. The bullet then went through an inside wall and ricocheted off the chimney in the living room.

What I did not realize during the 1930s and 1940s, my growing-up years, was that conditions for blacks had not progressed, given the proliferation of antiblack slurs, slights, plain prejudices, jokes, and stereotypes. It was a time when a staunchly prosegregationist newspaper freely printed the word "nigger" and referred to those white people who stood for civil rights as "nigger lovers."

Years later I learned, the hard way, of the terrible costs exacted upon black people during those times. The 1930s were a terrible time, if for no other reason than that black children were denied an education; this caused an immense trauma to be paid for in future years with "black blood and souls and minds." I realize now that the land we rented when I was a kid kept us in the middle of "land, land all over" but left us landless.

But I also realize again and again that our rented farm was somewhat of a world away from the real world for all my family. Our world as young children was a very special world. A peaceful place. And for us kids, all the world was black.

The day before I was born, I am told that Papa had to hurry up and get Lena Talbert to come help Mama in a real big hurry. Papa had to quickly hitch up the buggy that was kept under the shed built off the hay barn, and make the three-hour round trip at breakneck speed and bring back Nurse Talbert, the area's noted midwife. I was born the next morning to Chalmers and Eva Archer, at the Place, near Tchula, Mississippi. I was their firstborn.

I often mention that the first thing I remember about the Place was the back door of our house and my initial experience of meeting the snake in the cotton field behind it. That event surely must have been one of the most vivid, but there are many other snapshots—images—to recall as well. One was the road home from Rose Hill, the church school that I went to along with Mama when I was about five years of age. Mama was a teacher there.

A large wild possum grapevine grew up the bank on one side of the road and a sweet grapevine up the other bank. This was just before you started up the hill to the Place proper. The whole area was striking by the stretch of any imagination, in all seasons. But in the spring, everything on the road up the hill and on the Place was bright, and fresh, and new, and completely blooming with small trees, berries, plums, and other bushes. There was no gravel on the road for wet times, and the road up the hill was quite a challenge. The hill had special significance for all of us on the Place.

I remember so well how the road up the long hill with the tall banks on each side was not wide enough for two cars or wagons or any other vehicles to pass. You could not see the bottom from the top or the top from bottom. So, before anyone started up or down, it was the practice to call out a warning. If at the top, one would yell "coming down" or if at the bottom, "coming up."

The right rear wheel of a wagon going down was always chained securely to the wagon bed to slow down the vehicle. So, it was always the wagon going up that had to retreat. But there was still a big problem for the retreating wagon, because it was difficult to pilot backward with a spirited team of mules on a steep hill with sharp curves. But all in all, our hill-road was a "happy" one. It was a lovely road, and as a little child, I always loved to look at the vine-covered banks, as if they were a special tapestry woven just for me.

At the top of the hill, the pastures were grass-covered and rolling, and no description could do justice to their loveliness. The grass was rich and green and so thick it was matted. You could not see the ground. You could look out on some of the fairest fields in central Mississippi. And in the early evenings, soon after we reached home from school, you could hear the music of mockingbirds and many other birds. Those were such cheerful and reassuring sounds for a young boy.

As you approached the Place during the spring in the 1930s, you smelled the damp humus and the black earth turned by plows. The fields contrasted with the ever present cypress swamps at the bottom of the hill. I remember the fragile new green leaves of the sweet gum trees, and the tupelo trees. It seemed that there were always warm breezes during the spring months. Although I did not realize it during my younger years, the Place was still an antebellum-frontier-homestead type of settlement.

There were the ever present horses and mules pulling plows, with male family members in straw hats and overalls planting seeds for the summer's harvest. More often than not, families made a bale of cotton—or two tall wagon beds full of corn—to the acre. Those agricultural feats equaled any in the South at the time. Hay, fruit orchards, truck gardens, and other crops were bountiful.

The first home to be sighted at the crest of the road, at the north end top of the hill, was Cousin Ellis Booker's house. His was the typical rural home of renters in Mississippi in about 1935. Farther on were some cabins, mostly log structures, but the homes were mostly built-over, added-to structures left over from the days of slavery.

Close by Cousin Ellis's house was a molasses mill which he used to cook sorghum and Louisiana cane juice into delicious Louisiana syrup and thick brown sorghum molasses for us all. This was much like the molasses mills on plantations in earlier days.

I remember so well the stripped and creosoted logs embedded in the side of the banks only a short distance from the gate leading to the north section of the Place. Now as I look back, the gate, never locked, was a symbol of a way of life. It was representative of a self-sustaining black community. Something to be quite proud of in the 1930s. At any time, for that matter.

There was not much difference between our habits on the Place in the 1930s and white people's during slavery time. But unlike the situation for blacks in that earlier period, everybody on the Place was free, and in our own small community pretty much in charge of his or her day-to-day life. Still, many of the antebellum traditions were continued.

We happily carried on the Christmas traditions of white slave owners of years gone by. Early in December it became time for Christmas baking. Our family prepared all kinds of cakes, pies, and other delicious desserts and sweet courses. Spicy molasses cookies and warm cider were served to all guests.

About the same time, the houses on the Place were dressed up for the holidays. Decorations included red ribbons, homemade wreaths of cedar and glossy magnolia leaves. Homemade Christmas candles lit the homes—as well as the outbuildings—as in past antebellum celebrations. Cornshuck dolls were made, and everyone had apples from stores in Tchula town.

During the holidays, many women wore long sweeping gowns and colorful turbans. Why, I don't know, but the practice might have evolved from festive occasions in our African past.

Christmas carolers went from door to door, singing bygone hymns of the season. And, yes, Santa came to our house and most of the houses around.

In the kitchen of Uncle Perry's home—a large house that once was the plantation's big house—fruits from his harvest were cooked for the holiday season. Everybody visiting at this time of year, from on the Place and off, was offered a taste of the dish on the stove; they were also invited to share the meal. Sometimes, it was a humble meal of corn bread, greens, peas, or stew. Other times it was hot biscuits sopped with molasses.

Usually Aunt Esther or Uncle Perry would greet us at the front door of their home. Aunt Esther, who was quite young in those days, was said to be "as delicate as a magnolia fragrance on a spring breeze." There was usually someone at the back of Uncle Perry's house to help out. Uncle Perry was considered the leader and most important person on the Place.

In true accordance with past southern tradition, if the family was a large one, the boys slept in the house until they were six to eight years old. Then they went to an outbuilding usually built close to the main house. Girls stayed in the house until they were married. Uncle Nick's was really the only family in our settlement that used an outbuilding for this purpose, but Uncle Perry's house also had one, although his family was much too small to need the building.

So many little things to notice, and to remember. Like hoppers. The hoppers were where ashes were collected for making lye soap. There was one at every house. There were also smokehouses at all the homes for keeping meats, and cottonhouses all around for storing cotton until it could be taken to the gin.

There were two double outhouses across the backyard from Uncle Perry's house. Around the outhouses were trellises, covered during summer with roses hiding the buildings. Some distance from his house, there were large barns with wagon sheds. There were also smaller barns near our house, Uncle Nick's, and some other houses.

We really did not depend on the outside world for much of

anything. For us, self-sufficiency was the order of the day for everything but religion and education.

For instance, Uncle Nick was a shining example of self-sufficiency. Not only did he put in many hard hours at his smithy, he also doubled as candlemaker and potter. Sure, coal oil lamps were common, but many households still used candles to provide light. And Uncle Nick's skillful hands caressed wet lumps of clay into necessary dishes and other appliances for use on the Place.

Above all, dreams assured us that there were forever ways out of indifference, hand wringing, and despair. Papa said that there were "lights in all of the children's eyes." That light, he said, "would always enable them to see the future and have courage."

That was important to remember in the late summers, under the broiling hot sun, working the dusty fields. When pulling heavy cotton sacks among the tall cotton stalks. When stooping along the rows to reach the open cotton bolls. When being scratched by briars and by nettles that escaped the cotton chopper's hoes.

It all made for hard workdays summer after summer. Year after year. But it remained important to cherish the light in children's eyes.

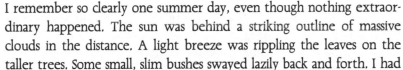

I remember so clearly one summer day, even though nothing extraordinary happened. The sun was behind a striking outline of massive clouds in the distance. A light breeze was rippling the leaves on the taller trees. Some small, slim bushes swayed lazily back and forth. I had spent much of the day glancing hopefully at the clouds, gauging their movements, willing the rain to come, in vain.

As the oldest child in the family, I was given responsibility for the farm's truck crop. We desperately needed a good truck crop each year for sale to people in Tchula. This was especially true in the 1930s. Money from the garden was needed to buy such things as sugar, flour, clothes, and supplies for school.

To raise a fine garden, we needed rain. We often talk now about how we kids would linger by the cistern, walk the dew-wet turn rows on quiet farm mornings, and keep looking up at the Mississippi sky.

That day, as usual, we stared into the distance. About a quarter of a mile to the west of our house, garden, and fields was a high hill far enough and high enough to be awe inspiring yet close enough to feel connected to our land and, somehow, to us. It was on this hill that all of us young folk kept our eyes fixed during that day.

For one reason, we thought the hill might be a magnet for rain clouds. Another reason is the story of Ben's Death. In about 1910, Ben, a young black man who lived on the nearby plantation, close to the site where we now had our largest cornfield, stole a hog and some flour to feed his hungry family. That night, the plantation owner at the time, and his Klan followers, took Ben from his cabin to the infamous Tchula jail. The cabin was then burned along with its meager contents, and Ben's family was put off the plantation with no place to go. (Our Uncle Perry took the family in until they were able to join family and friends in Detroit.) That same evening, Ben was tried by six white men and found guilty. He was forced to confess. The plantation owner himself used a broadax to decapitate the accused. The unfortunate victim's head was mounted on a stick and placed in the plantation owner's family's graveyard not too far from the big plantation house.

The unearthly sight was left in the graveyard as a warning to other black people. We kids were told that the stick and skull *were still there*. As for the plantation owner, he died a tragic death in his own house. Some said that he was poisoned by a close member of his family. Some said by a friend. But in the black community the word was that he was poisoned by one of his black cooks.

Both the graveyard and the plantation house sat on the peak of the hill that riveted our attention. Although our farm's fields dipped and rolled, sometimes abruptly, there was no point from which the hill, Ben's hill, could not be seen. It was the most prominent thing in the area. That hill had a very distinct place in all of our daily lives. We often thought about Ben's head still on watch there, a baleful sentry, almost a sacred one.

On that summer afternoon, the sky darkened many miles beyond the hill and the faint boom of thunder could be heard. So we studied this big natural barrier even more earnestly and even talked to it. There was that "human" hill—Ben's hill!—and our mind games.

The question of the day was whether the storms would be strong enough to push over the hill and bring merciful rain to the almost parched beds of my personal truckpatch. Or even if the hill would be generous enough to let the rain move on through.

Precious little rain had made it past the hill-wall in June, and the whole bunch of us took to blaming the hill for the lack of rain. On more days than not, the heavy black clouds gathered behind the hill and then simply scattered. We often looked to the south to see the sheets of rain driving down. We could then look to the far north and see a similar picture.

We children sometimes imagined that the hill was a great big dam, and for some unknown reason, was in just the right place to prevent the thunderstorms that seemed to fall everywhere but where we wanted them: on our garden.

Then there were times when we made the hill into something human, or more than human. We imagined that it was somehow a judge and disciplinarian, holding back the rain clouds as punishment for something we did wrong. At other times, though, we decided the clouds were held back because of something black people had done. It was Ben's fault! Or, the lack of rain was the revenge of the malevolent plantation owner on his cook.

Some nights, deep in sleep, we dreamed about rains and floods. We saw withering plants coming back alive from hard downpours and saw browning fields turn beautiful green again.

Those were the games that our minds played when the need for moisture was desperate. We knew that it should not have been that way. We were told from birth that "only God could change the weather." But we children could not come to terms with this fact. We could never quite understand that there was nothing we could do but accept our lot.

We relied heavily on the almanac and other signs. Our hopes for rain rose and fell accordingly. Through June of that year, the almanac had predicted some afternoon showers, but they did not come. First we blamed the almanac and then the hill. We just knew that the local belief was true, that Ben's hill manipulated the weather in order to drive us off the land.

The truth was that June and July, more often than not, would be dry months in Tchula, Mississippi, and there was nothing to be done except bring up water from the pond. Or haul water from the creek below the hill on a one-mule sledge we made ourselves. But whatever went on, we always had one eye cocked toward the hill.

The season was half over. The lettuce flourished from ample early rain but petered out with the heat—as always. The broccoli did well, was cut, and the fall crop of seedlings was growing fast in Papa's makeshift greenhouse. The snap peas were finished, and now the green beans were in full flower but were desperate for more water.

We went through the usual anticipation of searching for, eating, and selling the first of our June-ripened tomatoes, tastier from the heat, and we thrilled at the sight of peppers and eggplants forming on the bushes.

We children watched as the squash and melons—at least those that survived the cutworms and our seed-robbing crows—were pushing out into the rows. The pumpkins were doing passably well. The potatoes were forming nicely in their hilled rows. All of these were signs that we would be able to make many trips into town to "peddle" our wares. We would have lots of vegetables to sell.

We children usually spent a lot of time speculating about everything regarding our garden and the hill. But the thought sometimes occurred to us that perhaps we paid too much attention to the hill. Putting too much blame on it. And perhaps not paying enough attention to the garden itself.

All of this we knew. Yet the next morning, with the first light of dawn, the first thing we did was look up at the hill to see if it was still there and to search for a nearby rain cloud.

Our little mind game again, and it was easy to forget that it was July and nothing could change the rain patterns. The hill was still there, not a cloud could be seen, and not much else was new that day on the Place. Nothing happened that day, and yet a little of everything. Most of all, we thought about Ben, up on that hill.

The Depression was terrible for everybody, but black renters like us probably felt hard times less than any other group in central Mississippi.

At least that was true for those of us living on the Place. This was a fact because a small amount plus nothing still equals a small amount. I remember the lament that Bluesman Lonnie Johnson sang: "Hard time don't worry me, I was broke when it started out." He told the story in song quite well.

Poverty was already a way of life for most black people when the bottom fell out of the farm economy in the 1920s. In central Mississippi, black people had already learned to "stretch a nickel a mile." Better than many other people.

Most of the people around us were sharecroppers or lived on plantations under even worse arrangements. Central Mississippi was very rural and very poor country. We on the Place were, at best, working poor. Black people as a whole learned a whole lot about survival as they went from the slave block to a dubious freedom.

I remember quite well the Depression days, as I look at some old photographs given to me by my cousin Tommie Archer, Uncle Nick's son. The photos were taken during those times. I find that looking at the old photos is a great way to re-create history in my mind, and to better understand the complex and ambiguous reality of black conditions, values, and aspirations during those difficult years.

Look at one old snapshot, for example, and see again the black pots in the yards used to make hominy from corn and to make lye for cleaning. You can see the daily rhythms of everyday life in this picture. Other pictures bring to memory the unkind treatment of laborers and hired farmhands in our rural southern society during the 1930s. A picture of Uncle Nick's house, taken by Tommie, gives me the opportunity to remind myself that black families seldom had the white picket fences, neatly mowed lawns, and clapboard houses depicted in Hollywood films of the era. The black American experience, including the history of poverty, extreme segregation, exclusion, and discrimination, reverberates in photographs of those years. There is ready evidence, too, of poor health and a lack of education. It is all there.

Yes, the pictures show a difference between a simplistic idea of poor people and past black life, and a more complex and mysterious reality of blacks as people in the South in the 1930s. And Cousin Tommie's photos relate to signs of cultural and historical forces and the results of growth and decay. All family albums are valuable in this regard. A collection of old snapshots becomes an archive of American history, as well as a chronicle of a family.

I found, though, that the one major requirement for effective observations and conclusions about the Depression, of course, is to have "lived through it all." The pictures pointed out, in black and white, the real situation of Mississippi black people. They also showed, I think, that even though we were poor, we were not spiritually poor. There was also faith and hope in the people's eyes.

Visitors from the North and other places in the 1930s gave us an excellent opportunity for comparing poor black people in Tchula and Lexington with those in Chicago, Memphis, and other places that "homed" a large number of us. We were able to compare and judge the degree of well-being enjoyed in many other areas. Employment in textile mills, tobacco factories, and other manufacturing industries paid such low wages, we were often told by our relatives, that those in the urban areas remained poor by any definition of the word.

These visitors also told us that good workers in the North had no assurance of employment or of fair wages. But if they were able to find work, their income was indeed somewhat higher than ours in the South. The average wages of hired hands in the 1930s—if and when they were able to find work at all—in Mississippi was about eight dollars a month. This salary included lodging, boarding, washing, and mending. If workers paid their own expenses, they earned about fifty-five cents a day. Pay was about 10 percent higher in the North and a bit more in some other areas.

Yet here again there were surprising anomalies. In Tchula and Lexington, many black people, especially renters, ate meat two to three times a day. There often could be meat on the table even when money was tight. This was because most people raised the animals providing the meat. If meat had to be bought, it was less expensive than in other parts of the country. Fatback was eight to ten cents a pound. Chickens were sold at thirty-five to fifty cents each. Wild game was free. If bought, it was very cheap. Beef was reasonable.

During the Depression whiskey was cheap, but still cost something, and those men who were heavy drinkers often spent a considerable portion of their family's income on whiskey. Many families grew their own tobacco, but store-bought tobacco was cheap and not taxed. Most men, and some women, used chewing tobacco and smoke pipes.

It was a sad era for black women on plantations during the Depression. On the plantation next door to the Place, one could look at the poor physical conditions of wives, daughters, and other females. It was they who were indeed "slaves" of the day. Looking later at pictures from the times, I could readily see that the life many women led was one of hardship, deficiency, and unremitting hard labor.

It was rare to see a woman on a plantation during the Depression who reached the age of thirty without losing every trace of youth and beauty. You continually saw women with infants on their knees who you thought were their grandchildren until told otherwise. Even the young girls, though often with lovely features, looked sick, thin, and exhausted. Very seldom did you see a healthy female on plantations. Women seldom laughed and seldom were they plump.

Even women working off the plantations in the 1930s had lives with bleak prospects. Many spent lifetimes in domestic service. This work had the reality of slavery, and any benefits achieved by the labor unions in that era missed them altogether. Since daughters were an extension of mothers, in most cases they were, in the full sense of the word, also domestic slaves. For a black woman, domestic service was often her only opportunity, her sole source of income, the only job in town.

"Let any man's son be equal to any other man's son" was a popular slogan of the day. But did we think it might apply to daughters too? Or grandmothers?

Mama Lucy was our grandmother on our mother's side. Our grandmother was small and trim of figure, a real wisp of a woman and cute as a button. She was light-brown complexioned with a full head of straight black hair.

Mama Lucy was the one who told us all about her "old days" and tales of her parents when they were slaves. She told us about how her parents were not permitted to get married. And how her mother under slavery could not even claim as hers the children she gave birth to, for they too were the property of her master.

Mama Lucy's mother had told her that "when freedom came around

1865, hunger became the topmost worry of former slaves." There was no certainty whatsoever in the postwar South. This, her mother said, "was real rough because nobody cared about or listened to former slaves' problems. At least during the days of slavery," Mama Lucy was told, "there was always food, clothing, and shelter." Freedom did bring a new set of challenges, but food without freedom would never satisfy. Mama Lucy knew this. She had no desire to return to the past.

In no way could Mama Lucy be thought of as old-fashioned. She was someone who was well ahead of the times. She was a terrific grand-mother.

She was born in the Mount Olive area near Tchula, and married Malachi Rutherford and lived in Vicksburg for a short time. Mama Lucy was the mother of four daughters: our mother (Eva), an older daughter (Edna), and two younger daughters (Rebecca and Dixie). Rebecca and Dixie were her children by Mama Lucy's second husband, Richard Parham of Lexington.

Our grandmother talked to us about things like the splendor of a quiet summer day, when the heat was at its most intense and when one worked one's way across the dusty cotton fields, thirst dominating one's thoughts and philosophy. From experience such as this, she said, "one learns well that water is the substance of life."

She told us about how "we all are creatures of the earth," and how much she enjoyed it as she felt the freshly turned farm soil between her toes, when she was a young girl and even in her later years. She told us how she loved the scent of the fields after a rain.

Mama Lucy was sometimes even outrageous and daring. She had dreams and hopes for black people, and she was aware of those dreams and hopes like no other person I ever knew. And she was one who never felt sorrow for herself, nor would she let us feel sorry for ourselves. Many a family tree has been strengthened by the spunk of a grandmother like Mama Lucy.

I believe that there is no better way to experience the past than through food. As a young teenager, I got the smoke of Mama Lucy's outside fire into my face and hair and felt the pull of my muscles as I helped her move the heavy pots. It was something to experience our grandmother's array of foods, as well as the tradition, sociability, and down-home enjoyment associated with them. Mama Lucy breathed the lives of our people into her foods.

Our grandmother usually gave us kids a breakfast of scrambled eggs with fresh herbs, country sausage, salad, and spoon bread—a puffed-up corn bread marvel. Spoon bread is a black dish of simple elegance that was passed down from the days when slave women "made up recipes for their white families."

As was the custom among black people during those times, Mama Lucy's country cooking of corn bread knew no season. She did not put any special importance on corn bread—it was simply good. Mama Lucy usually made it every day. Often in the form of batter cakes, mostly called hoecakes, with the basic ingredients being flour and meal. Her batter cakes were mixed, poured, flipped, and on the table in short order. Hot with lacy crisp edges and served with whole milk and buttermilk.

The hoecakes, which we ate as children and still eat today when at home, continue to have salt and milk added to the batter. They are cooked pancake-style in a heavy skillet or on a griddle. A little vegetable shortening or oil is put in the pan or the griddle just before cooking the cakes. A few drops of oil is also poured into the batter.

Batter cakes went well with the beans, peas, and squash that often made up Mama Lucy's simple but mouth-watering southern meals. Then there was her cornmeal, which went into dressing for her holiday turkey or roasted chicken. And the corn sticks that she "fed up" with vegetable soup or stew, and, sometimes—to our delight—golden muffins for breakfast. "All of this," she said, "is in the black tradition of corn bread 'meals' and still is talked about here in Mississippi."

Mama Lucy explained to us that corn bread is a warming, refreshing food—easy to make and inexpensive. She always made it clear, as we already knew so well, that corn bread is as good with fresh vegetables in the summer and fall as it is with steaming stew on a cold, damp February day. "It is a real, real black food," she always told us. "And good for you," she would go on.

Mama Lucy told us about how her mother, who was affectionately called Summa, also made delicious home-cooked corn bread. The bread was made with a mixture of cornmeal and water, formed into small cakes. It was known in those days as "pone." Simple corn bread is called by that name today. Summa also passed on to Mama Lucy the fact that hoecakes were merely pone, getting their name from the practice of slaves cooking the simple bread on the blade of straight hoes or shovels thrust into the fireplace or on the hearth.

Summa was supposedly freed when the Thirteenth Amendment was approved in 1865. She was still very much alive during my childhood, and when I was a little boy she would hold me on her lap and tell me her history. Summa told me one day, "I am not certain when I was freed, because all slaves were not freed at the end of the Civil War." She told me once, too, about the Fourteenth Amendment which was approved in 1868 to protect the rights of freed slaves. She also often mentioned the Fifteenth Amendment, which she said was approved around the year 1870. "It did not grant equal justice to all citizens," she said. She also told me that "neither black nor white women had the right to vote until 1920." I did not understand all of this at the time. Summa was the only relative who actually experienced slavery with whom I remember having long talks about that horrible institution.

Summa told me, too, how black people made the first "hush puppy." One of her and Mama Lucy's favorite stories is about how this type of pone came about. The story goes that corn bread balls were fried alongside fish in makeshift containers by escaping slaves and tossed to barking dogs to keep them quiet. Summa also maintained that true hush puppy had to be cooked with fish, and only after one pan of fish was cooked in the oil. Otherwise, she said, the bread would not have the proper flavor.

On special occasions, Mama Lucy cooked tasty "crackling bread." This was done by adding cracklings to basic pone batter. Cracklings were bits of crisp meat that were left after boiling fat meat to make lard. We made them in big black pots in our barnyard by cooking small cubes of slab bacon or freshly killed salt pork. Water was added to the meat being boiled until most of the fat was cooked out and the bits of meat were crisp. Crackling bread was delicious with soup, cooked greens, and peas.

Now, another special corn bread dish Mama Lucy made for us children was cornmeal mush. She made it by bringing water to boil and stirring in cornmeal. When the mixture finished cooking, she let it cool and sliced it. She then reheated it and gave it to us with syrup and butter, or alongside eggs and sausages. Mama Lucy sometimes added pork products to the mush and it became "scrapple." This was a special treat too.

Besides Mama, Mama Lucy was the best cook in the world! But after all, Mama learned to cook from Mama Lucy.

One day in spring during the late 1930s a heavy storm blew through. A light tornado touched down just east of Jackson. Near Greenwood, about thirty-six miles from the Place, about four inches of rain fell. In Holmes County, over two inches fell. It was springtime, and lots of rain was sometimes good news and sometimes bad news for farmers. All of this I remember distinctly. As a poor black farm kid, I had a stake in these matters.

This particular night after the big storm, I along with my family returned home by buggy from a wedding. We attended the affair at the Mount Zion Baptist Church. Ordinarily, the distant lights of farmyards and rutted dirt roads kept our attention, and we would stick to familiar roads. But that night we took a shortcut. A new way home. The storm had cleared the air, and left a sense of adventure in its aftermath.

The moon came out, and it shone off the muddy water that pooled in the fields and was hissing down the sides of embankments along the road as we passed Aunt Sally's house. As the houses continued to thin and trees thickened on both sides of the road, our spirits really lifted in anticipation and soon we came to a soothing view of a large pond, gleaming in the moonlight.

Then a bigger pond came into view through breaks in surrounding foliage. It was a silver beacon. We were on a road below a small dam with its cascading falls. Soon after we passed the Parist place, houses disappeared altogether. It was a quiet night except for the sounds of rivulets of water everywhere. Then the woods became lonely, and dark, and this went on for a mile or two. Deer were running that night. Maybe they were jumpy from the storm. They dashed in front of us constantly. Once a tiny fawn pranced down the road before us for a hundred yards or more. We only glimpsed but deeply sensed the presence of other wildlife. This was an area rich with rabbit, raccoon, squirrel, and turkey.

Several minutes past Aunt Statia and Uncle Cal Benjamin's place, we came out of the woods onto a small dirt road that led directly home. We then followed the road quietly to our house. It was a wonderful nighttime buggy ride of sparkling waterfalls, emerald foliage, and dancing fawns in the moonlight. It was a shortcut and new route for us, but Papa knew the way to the house like the back of his hand.

It took storms just like that one to completely disturb our regular farming routine. Some families would now replant their beans when and where they could. Others on the Place would think about sowing sorghum in the smooth patches where the corn got washed out. Those families who did not put drains in their low fields would once again consider doing so, adding the cost of backhoe and tile in their minds.

The rains earlier that year proved to be a mixed blessing for Tchula farmers. Big harvests for some crops, but low yields for others. May and June were particularly wet, holding back some seed planting and hay curing. But "after so many dry years, we can't complain," Papa said. Despite the fact that people talked a lot about choosing the best fertilizer and seed, "moisture is really what makes our crops," Cousin Ellis remarked. Corn and truck crops were bumper ones in our area and many other parts of Mississippi. It was the best year in five.

On the other hand, the increased volumes reduced prices, canceling out some of the benefits of bigger yields. Most farmers said that their cotton crops actually earned them more money in dry years. Still, many other factors also affected prices, including crop yields in places other than the South.

This particular wet year saw increased food supplies in the pastures for cattle and livestock. And, as I said, vegetable and plant growers were having an excellent year—despite their problems with insects and weeds. Said Uncle Perry, "It seems like every weed seed in the past forty years that never thought of sprouting, sprouted this year." Another difficulty was the drenching rains in the spring of that year. Although wet weather is usually good for corn and beans too, these spring rains had threatened to wash away both crops. Nevertheless, throughout Mississippi there was a payoff at harvest time. Families made a record yield of both corn and beans: fifty-three bushels of corn per acre, and twenty bushels of beans per acre.

Unfortunately, there were some problems with the hay crop. Wet weather is good for growing hay. It grew fast and vigorously that spring in Holmes County, but at gathering and curing time it was a nightmare. A stretch of about two weeks is needed for the hay harvest, but there was never more than a five- or six-day break in the rain. Some harvesting had to be delayed. But families on the Place simply cut down the tall grass with mowers so that usable hay could be cut later. Hay that was rained on during the curing process lost color and food value. It became susceptible to mold and rot. So it turned out to be somewhat of a bad year for hay.

The year was hard on our orchards, too. Many of the strawberry plants literally drowned while they were in blossom, and the berries that formed were small. Peaches were scarce throughout the state because of a late chill and frost. Most other stone fruit, such as plums and cherries, were so-so.

Dry years are the best for grapes and muscadines. But that year, surprisingly, grapes yielded a higher-than-normal production. On the other hand, fungus was a headache and got worse as the humidity rose.

So all and all, it was a good year and a bad year. Life on the Place went on as usual. Things were not too good, and yet not too bad for us renters. We had less than our white neighbors, but still were a whole world apart from the plantations. And it was wonderful to have an occasional magical buggy ride after a tornado.

6 Church and Plow, Bullets and Hope

Ghosts of the 1930s are all around me, tugging at my ear, nudging my memory. This is a story of things remembered, while I lived in Tchula, and later Lexington, Mississippi, during the 1930s and on up to 1955.

Times were tough all over. For all people. But for us black people of the town of Tchula, the 1930s and 1940s found us the "poorest of poor" as far as material wealth was concerned. It is hard to even describe the distress of black employment and the lack of it, the abysmal housing, the nation's worst schools, and the pitiful health care during those times. Those were the years of the worst black poverty, disease, illiteracy, and of wide racial inequities.

A Jackson, Mississippi, newspaper in February 1929 had printed these statements: "We, the white race, achieved everything that is worth while, and are divinely ordained as the better class of people." And: "We must maintain our 'integrity' in order to preserve the wonderful civilization earmarked by our 'Almighty.' And as Anglo-Saxons, Caucasians, and 'Christians,' it is necessary to set up insurmountable barriers to prevent the mixing of races." These attitudes didn't change much— if at all—in the next two decades.

Making a living in rural Mississippi has always been difficult for blacks. To my surprise, Grandfather Payton told Papa that, following slavery, white landowners initially adopted a relatively fair wage system of paying black laborers a definite amount in money for their services. By the day, month, or year. "But this was far too brief, as it was snuffed out in about twelve years," Grandfather Payton told my father.

My fraternal grandfather went on to tell how owners of large plantations decided that their interest could be better served in their then "shaky" conditions by adopting a system known as "tenancy." The freedmen had little choice in the matter. They were dependents who had to take whatever was offered to them, or become drifters or worse.

The practice of tenancy became strikingly similar to peonage, and slavery itself; tenancy was one of the worst evils southern black people were to suffer since slavery. Ordinarily, one thinks of tenants as persons paying for the use of property, but otherwise just as independent in their transactions as the owners of the property themselves. But for black farmers in Mississippi during the 1930s, this was usually far from the situation. In the first place, there were many different kinds of tenants, with varying degrees of independence and liberty depending on the specific contract signed with the landowners.

Altogether, there were five types of tenants: (1) share tenants paid a certain share of their crops for the use of the land but furnished their own work animals; (2) croppers resembled share tenants except that work animals were provided by the planters; (3) share-cash tenants paid rent partly in cash and partly in products; (4) cash tenants paid exclusively in cash for the use of the land; and (5) standing renters paid a stated amount of farm products for the use of the land. Of the five types, the croppers were the most dependent on landowners, and their will was subject almost completely to the landowners' will. The practice of the system was passed from one generation to the next.

In the 1920s, my father's family shared in a "family rent group" who were cash tenants of about six hundred acres of good cotton and corn land—"the Place," as it came to be called. The families at the Place were Uncle Perry's, Bro' John Davis's, Aunt Statia's, Uncle Nick's, Cousin Ellis's, Papa's, and a few others who were not related to us. Uncle Perry, the eldest, rented the Place for all. He was our patriarch.

Papa told the family one day in 1931 that President Hoover refused to admit that there was a Depression. "Good times are just around the corner," the president said. But our father knew better. Everyone on the Place also knew better. The stock market had collapsed about sixteen months earlier. But as long as we could plow, we on the Place had no plans to starve. But just the same, times were still hard all over.

This was the era of happy stereotypes, Aunt Jemima and Rastus, Little Black Sambo and Mammy. This was about the time when Hollywood producers wanted black people to be thought of as mammies, servants, nannies, and maids. Minstrels and buffoons also began to multiply. Those images were a few among many of the times. Tap-dancing blacks on the silver screen are a memory from the 1930s.

The movies were quick therapy for the Great Depression. But there were more pressing concerns. Like the involuntary servitude all around us. Involuntary servitude in the form of sharecropping and forced labor. One of the most pressing problems of the era for landlords was the challenge of keeping people on plantations. The owners simply could not make it without workers. They were dependent on cheap labor. Plantation owners resorted to coercions, constraints, pressures, and violence which was often supported by law.

As I noted, the roots of this evil go way back. About a dozen years after the Civil War ended, Mississippi established labor-by-vagrancy laws, whereby black families were compelled to work for someone and to continue to work for whatever pay was offered. These people were put to work on public highways or they were leased to planters. This was, in fact, actual slavery. According to our grandfather, the federal government tried to do something about this "new" slavery. The government tried to use free manhood suffrage in an attempt to curb this evil.

But after federal troops were withdrawn from the Deep South, the return to local rule gave the governing class an opportunity to fully disenfranchise blacks and remove black people from the political arena. It was then easy for whites to continue involuntary servitude from then on.

After federal troops were withdrawn, Mississippi put into place laws that in effect provided for "slavery" as a payment for debt. There were tight legal frameworks and southern rural customs to keep workers on the job. This did not make slavery legal as such, but landowners knew how to get around the letter of federal law by extreme tactics. Tactics in tandem with the local court procedures that effectively forced black people to stay in the service of landlords. These local laws penalized black people who failed to comply with contracts for work, preventing the defection of the laborers from their employers. The laws also provided for violations of contracts with a second party who assumed responsibility for debts, and for violations of acts of vagrancy.

What were black workers and families to do? How were they to endure? Answers were few and far between, and the solutions elude us to this day. However, throughout the Depression and the 1940s as well, we had two major sources of strength and hope. The family was one. The church was the other. Building on these two rocks, we knew our dreams would not die.

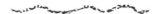

Think on these things. A summer evening fifty years ago. A time of respite, away from the plow. After the harsh Delta sun had moved west, beyond the Mississippi River, in the early evening there might be a gathering for a church supper. The place was Mount Olive Church near Tchula. The twentieth century had hardly made a dent on the tiny black community in that part of the state's remote northwestern corner. The nearest phone was in Tchula. People lived in shacks and log homes lighted with coal oil lamps, and they made do with outhouses, and slit trenches, and sometimes no facilities at all for personal hygiene purposes.

But those images are put aside for a while. We are remembering a church supper. Fresh faces, intelligent young faces. Old faces, courageous and tired faces. Hopeful faces. There were wiggly, eager kids. Proud parents, and their elders. There were the speckled porcelain cooking pans and black iron pots. And there was that energy of group expectancy, a congregation's shared anticipation, everyone looking forward to real enjoyment. Good clean merriment. Or maybe just an escape from the harsh reality of the time.

About forty or more people crowded around and inside the small church in a most impoverished community, deep in the Mississippi

cotton country. Dust rose in the late afternoon sunshine as wagons and
buggies moved along the winding road to the dead end between the
church and the graveyard. Mount Olive Church was a Baptist church.
All the churches that I knew of around Tchula at that time were
Baptist. Only in Lexington were there other denominations. My grandmother Mama Lucy's church in Lexington was an African Methodist
Episcopal Church.

Earlier on this southern Sunday, about noon, we sang three favorite
songs, "Steal Away," "The Old Rugged Cross," "Down by the Riverside,"
and other popular hymns. The lyrics, rhythm, and singing style of the
congregation demonstrated deep emotional enthusiasm and lots of rich
imagination. The church services were powerful, with an almost
ritualized intensity. Always, our prayers were for fair play, justice for all
people, and freedom from fear. We echoed President Roosevelt's
sentiments, and added our own.

The church services remain vivid in memory partly because of the
typical call-and-response participation that always took place between
the preacher and the congregation. There also was quite a bit of
shouting. And for us kids, the rigors and comforting patterns of the
traditional Sunday School. Bible verses to memorize, hymns to save us
from Sin, tales of scriptural heroes to emulate.

But what I remember most about an evening of a church supper
were the homemade wooden-handled, sharp paring knives made in
Uncle Nick's blacksmith shop. The tacked-down newspaper tablecloths,
homemade baseball caps, and funeral-parlor folding chairs. Dented
aluminum serving-pitchers full of lemonade, covered with moisture
from the ice bought at the icehouse in Tchula. And, of course, the
food itself. The simple, delicious, feasting pleasures of the vittles. All
under the shade trees. On the side of the church away from the
graveyard.

Mama brought in a bushel and a half of creek-cooled cucumbers for
the cucumber-and-onion salad. Uncle Nick picked the sweet corn the
night before from his patch. His was the large yellow corn, perfect for
getting your teeth into and then going down the row like a hay
mower.

Mr. Polk and Uncle Perry and Sis Mae and Aunt Fannie charcoaled the beef on a big outdoor smoker. In its former life, this homemade and ingeniously rigged smoker was a stainless-steel milk tank. It was sitting up on wheels, fairly glowing and trembling in its heat.

Cole slaw. Luscious cool and creamy cole slaw. Cabbage after cabbage went into the mix. It was made until about an hour or so before the meal.

Remember still more: watermelon pickles cool and spicy; zesty pumpkin butter, sweet almond apple butter, and tomato butter. Tart plum jam, and rich grapefruit-orange marmalade. Tomatoes and rolls and peas and greens and ribs and corn bread.

Dessert was peach sundaes: the peaches were peeled nearly within the half hour, the ice cream was served in many flavors and made up of little dips in small dishes. Homemade ice cream. You could have as much as you wanted. The pies and ambrosia were out of this world. Sister Booker made her pies from huckleberries picked from the woods.

Church suppers were happy and fun-filled affairs. But there was serious talk afterward. There was talk about the injustices all over. A lot of talk was about the black farmer who lost fifteen hundred acres of land near the church grounds. Good, rich, crop-producing land. A white plantation owner had paid the tax on the land for the number of years required by law, and by doing so, made the land his own.

The black farmer did not know that the taxes were not being paid in his name. There was nothing to be done. It was too late. The farmer was promptly put off the land. He and his family were allowed to take some furniture and clothes. But the mules and cows, farm equipment, and all the rest went to the new owner.

Many white landlords took advantage of uninformed black farmers and kept money that belonged to them. What to do about this? This was an important point of discussion at Sunday church suppers.

All too soon, it would be time to go. Good food and conversation came to a reluctant end. During the buggy ride home, we would pass an occasional one-room schoolhouse. A cabin. A barn. But mostly we looked at that amazing corn and cotton. Rows and rows of beautiful corn and cotton. All husbanded by black renters and owners. We looked at the pastures of Holstein and Jersey cows.

Snapshots: we see Mrs. Beatie Johnson sweeping her yard with a homemade broom, plucking up every blade of grass before it scarcely poked its way through the bare dirt "floor" outside her front door. Summertime, and she is wearing some very old worn-out sneakers. She amuses herself by singing her favorite hymn, "Nearer My God to Thee," while she works.

Tchula Lake was listless and olive green in the summer overcast evenings. Whenever we drove past the lake, my gaze and imagination would always be pulled to it. It was my lake, dark and sinister on a summer night but promising a boy many adventures. Then we would pass a place that once made buggies and was a passenger stop on the main L & N line just a few years before. It was always a long ride home, after a brief but happy time. It was the end of a good day. Or perhaps a brief escape.

In April 1940 we learned about a contemptible incident. Sarah Wilson's family was in bed one spring night when a shotgun blast riddled the front door of their house. A second blast sprayed peelers into the front bedroom. The attack was not totally unexpected—her father had attended a number of civil rights gatherings. The father had also taken the daring and dangerous step of "going down to the courthouse to register" to vote.

The event, as I look back on it, changed forever the life of the tall, reserved teenager Sarah, who was considered by the people in the community to be the nicest girl they knew. On that night, Sarah recalled many years later, "it became clear to me that anything could happen." After that, her interest in the civil rights movement changed from youthful curiosity to a full-time commitment.

My cousin Rezell and I also had a very different outlook on civil rights after learning what had happened to Sarah's family. We both made a decision to "be more mature in our thoughts and actions." So there certainly were, sometimes, indirect rewards as a result of frightful incidents. The shooting at the Wilsons' house, which fortunately caused no injuries, was just one of many such incidents that fueled the fight to better the lives of black citizens in the Mississippi Delta, in the Deep South, and throughout America.

About the same time, I also became fully aware that it was our family's and the community's contention that black people themselves should be front-runners in the fight for equality. My father made a short speech to a community group one evening. Rezell and I listened to his talk. Afterward we thought a lot about the group discussion that followed. This was the gist of Papa's message, taken from his personal papers:

> Yes, many of our people on plantations around us are starving, beaten, and forced to suffer unspeakable torment. What we have here is a struggle, together, to change an entrenched economic and political system defended by violence. We must continue to work hard to help ourselves. We must also work for success so we can represent the spirit of achievement and a success which we want to be found in our children in days to come. We must preserve our honor and pride. We must work hard for some very special qualities—vision, creativity, commitment, perseverance, compassion, and leadership—that will make us good role models for our children and people everywhere.
>
> Yes, we must set the example. Because our children are going to set the pace and help direct the focus on farms, businesses, government, and the whole nation during the years to come. We must strive to teach them the very best we can from kindergarten to college. Education is the thread that ties together all stages of life. These young folk are our future. We as a people must continue to live and survive and prosper. But let us not forget, as always, our achievements and our children's achievements in the future must remind us of our responsibility to ourselves.
>
> Yes, we must be front-runners. Someday we will be able to choose, be able to do and act as a free individual and people. And our aims must continue to be toward improving the future for all people. We all know that life is rough for black people right now, and our children are suffering. But there is nothing that we can't overcome, if we work together. With the right planning and if we expand our imaginations we can go far. We must work toward creative solutions to our problems. Let's look to the future, and endure. Let's all work hard. We can make it a creative adventure.

On the corner of my parents' bedroom mantel was always displayed a unique ring. It was given to Papa by a longtime friend. The ring was made from a spoon by a friend who had served time as a prisoner on the notorious Holmes County chain gang during the early 1920s.

The ring's shape was fashioned by hours of beating the spoon against brick or other hard metal. Father's friend was a member of a small group from Tchula who went to Lexington to protest the black voting situation of the times. As a result, he served three years and seven months in prison.

The friend who made the ring gave it to my father as a token of thanks for Papa's efforts to get him released. The attempts, he said, helped to make life bearable. "I wish to thank you," he told Papa, "on behalf of all my friends in prison and for myself, our heartfelt thanks to you for your efforts on our part." Four protesters were still on the chain gang at the time our family friend was released.

One of those who was still in jail during the same time, but released later, was Gransbill Williams. He came by to see us about twenty years later in Lexington. Papa showed him the ring. He looked at it in silence for a few moments. He then said, with so very much emotion, how well he remembered that particular ring. For a time the friend and he slept next to each other while on the gang. Mr. Williams told us about the horrors of prison. "We were usually shackled to twenty- to fifty-pound iron weights. Those were very hard times. There was so much humiliation. And sometimes death."

During that visit, he told us about the many abuses and police-station torture. For a time, too—every day they were in prison—he said that they wondered if the awful system that locked them away would ever be better. Mr. Williams's answer to that—almost twenty years later—was a skeptical "Yes, someday."

Released from prison, Mr. Williams regarded himself a lucky man, partly because of the work my father and others did on his behalf. In the 1930s and 1940s, thousands of black people remained on chain gangs and on county farms in the state of Mississippi. It was simply beyond belief how black people were arrested and held. However, Gransbill Williams knew. He had been there.

Mr. Williams also told us about a eighty-six-year-old man who was arrested for associating with the "wrong" people. He also told us about a sixteen-year-old black girl who was tortured and raped by police at the time she was arrested. He went on to say that there were more than one hundred prisoners on his particular gang while he was there and that "virtually no one escaped the gang" or "the horror and degradation of torture."

Mr. Williams said that medical care was still unknown twenty years later, and that entire gangs still died of diseases such as meningitis. He said that he also believed that shackle poison was still killing prisoners. Shackle poison, he told us, "was an infection caused by the constant rubbing of ankle irons on the legs of prisoners. Horrible and painful death," he said.

Mr. Williams recited the standard prison prayer for us. It went like this:

> We pray that our heavenly Father will bless and protect the families we left behind. We pray that somebody will remember that we are here and do something for us. We pray that we don't die of hunger, too much work without food and proper clothing, or of the beatings. We pray that we don't give up and cause harm to ourselves by self-inflicted mutilations such as hamstringing. We pray that none of us have to go to the sweatbox. We pray that someday we can go home to our families and loved ones.

If anyone tried to escape and was caught, Mr. Williams told us, he was put "in a coffinlike sweatbox, beaten, or riveted to twenty-five- to fifty-pound iron weight shackles. The same thing happened if we did not work hard or fast enough."

Church suppers and chain gangs. Snapshots. Gunfire. The sound of a certain hymn. As I think about some of my first church meetings, they become some of the most memorable times of my life. The "Regular" Sundays for preaching and all-day meetings were important, for one thing, because we got a chance to wear our Sunday outfits. Church was the social event of the week. There was Sunday school, then church. The most special meeting days of all were Baptism Sundays.

While we lived in Tchula, we went to Rose Hill Church most of the time, but at other times we went to Mount Olive. Rose Hill was about three miles from home. Mount Olive about five or six miles away.

During services, the preacher's message was always in the form of "sing-song" chants. The message was a "feeling." The sermon began with a statement of the day's text. The earliest text I remember was "We are like the tree planted beside the river's water." The Reverend

Clenton L. Clark, a young preacher from Lexington, was the pastor at
Rose Hill. His sermons were glorious. The Reverend Clark still lives in
Lexington, Mississippi.

As the preacher got further into the text, a feeling began to come
over us all. The whole congregation became a part of the sermon. The
preacher would begin to chant his lines, the words and rhythm more
and more like poetry. The timing, lulls, gaps, and hesitations became
more and more regular and harmonious. And as the congregation
became more and more anointed with the Holy Spirit, the reverend's
sermons would slide into song. What we all really did was chant the
word of God after the preacher and often along with him.

The Sunday church meetings were highly emotional. They started at
a low pitch in intensity and progressed to a high level of spiritual
passion. All of this was, and still is, expressed by the gradual change
from when the text was given, through a phase of chanting, and on to
highly emotional singing.

In the 1930s, most black preachers were excellent singers. The
Reverend Clark was no different. Most ministers grew up in homes in
which music played a big role, in the family and in the church. So most
preachers had a sense of music, and its rhythms, tempo, sounds, and
beats. We all responded to the sermon, songs, and chantings with
unrestrained emotions. Usually our responses were "Amen," "Thank
you, Jesus," and "Tell the truth!" I did not understand all of this at the
time, but I could follow the crowd's leads as well as the grown-ups.

During the particular service that I remember now, the Reverend
Clark had us all aroused to feel, most definitely, the Spirit of the Lord.
We could hear individual cries throughout the congregation. Some of
Rose Hill's members lost consciousness. Some danced in the aisles,
seemingly involuntarily. The preacher was equally excited. Some of the
ladies laughed, some cried unashamedly. When the services were over,
everybody said that they had a happy time. These outpourings were
our path to rejoicing, and to renewed inner strength.

One day when we had the Reverend Clark to dinner, he talked
about religion. He explained that preachers did not need notes during
their sermons. The reason was, he said, "that the Holy Ghost uses us to
bring the message to church members."

Papa once mentioned that the heritage of black preachers influenced the style of their performances and of the congregation's responses. He felt that the African folksong culture of call-and-responses was a special heritage of black people. Not only was it the preacher who was directly in line with this African tradition, but during the holy services, all of us were free to call out to the preacher, or to one another as the Spirit moved us.

Papa offered this explanation about the special role of black churches: "Take at Eastertime," he told me after I became older. "Like most, we flock to churches on Easter Sunday because the message of Easter gives us hope. But in our world, the black world, Easter is so very special because there is so much death. We hoped back in the 1930s, during the Depression, that we could see life in the midst of death," he said. He added that black people always longed to know, "What is the meaning of life here in our bondage, in these troubled times?" The little country churches in rural Mississippi provided the message of hope.

During a later sermon at his church, our Uncle Perry talked about the last words Jesus spoke on the cross before he was crucified. His sermon that day was "The Seven Last Words of Christ." That Sunday, with word and song, the congregation strived to give life to the following phrases: "Father forgive them, for they know not what they do. Verily I say unto you, today you shall be with Me in paradise. Women behold thy son; why has thou forsaken Me? I thirst. Father, into thy hands I commend my spirit. It is finished."

Uncle Perry told us that "the word is to let black people know that Jesus is the resurrection and in Him there is life." This was Uncle Perry's "regular" Easter Sunday message. It was a light in the darkness for black people at the time.

One thing for sure, I and the rest of the congregation were moved during these preaching services. Perhaps it was due to feelings flavored by the experience of living in the rural South. Or due to black people's common beliefs. Or the influence of our African roots and folk heritage.

Whatever the reasons, the feelings were truly there, and they sustained us.

7 Our Aunt Mama Jane

 We all remember ever so well what the preacher said at our aunt Mama Jane's funeral. "There will never be another like her. There will never be another Martha Jane Archer Jordan. Amen. Amen."

According to the records in the family Bible, Martha Jane (Mama Jane) Archer was born on the first day of November in 1872. She was only a year short of her one-hundredth birthday when she died in 1971. Mama Jane was the oldest of ten children born to Payton and Catherine Archer in what is called the Mount Olive community, situated approximately halfway between the hill town of Lexington and Delta town of Tchula in central Mississippi. All her brothers and sisters except her youngest brother, Chalmers, my father, always called her Sis' Jane. My father called her Mama Jane because he lived with her to continue his schooling soon after she was married. But she was always known as Mama Jane to later generations of the family too, because she was the oldest.

At the time of Mama Jane's birth, Reconstruction was in full swing in the Deep South. Her memories encompassed the reign of terror against freedmen in that era. And yet she persisted in her view that the Archer white folks—the family that had owned our grandfather and grandmother—were "the most benign of their generation." Hence, to us, she was indeed an anomaly.

Mama Jane's early childhood was spent on her uncle Perry's farm, where her family were tenants. Her formal education was practically nonexistent, although she attended the one-room school in Mount Olive Church. A single teacher taught grades one through eight at this school. Growing up on the farm, she learned how to do all the usual chores of farm women of that time.

From the time she was about eight years old, Mama Jane carried water to the field workers in a handmade cedar bucket, which was almost too heavy for her to carry when it was filled with water. She did this three or four times daily, carrying water from a creek, cistern, well, spring, or any such available source from as far away as a half mile or even more. "Sometimes in these creeks and springs frogs, scorpions, lizards, and snakes would have to be shooed away before I could dip up the water," Mama Jane often said.

"When I was not acting as water girl, I tended the younger children on the turn rows of the field, where they were usually left on spread-out homemade blankets called pallets." Turn rows are the narrow spaces left at the ends of crop rows for turning mule-and-horse-drawn or tractor-drawn plows and other implements so as not to damage the crops. These spaces usually did not have any shade or protection from the elements, so both she and her young charges suffered horribly from the heat and the cold at different times of the year.

At about ten or eleven years of age, Mama Jane began to chop and pick cotton, thin corn, and work in the family's vegetable garden throughout the growing season, which lasted from February through the Thanksgiving and Christmas holidays when the weather often became just too wretched for field work. Nevertheless, Mama Jane frequently spoke of times when the family picked cotton after the New Year when there was a good crop.

"In these so-called good years of the late 1880s, school was all but forgotten even for girls and women," Mama Jane said. "When the all important cotton had been picked, then the potatoes, corn, and other such crops had to be gathered. Even the women had to help pull the corn." Corn had to be pulled and piled for the wagons to come along and pick up. "When the women and young girls and boys didn't have to pull the corn, they were required many times to drive the wagon and load the corn," she would add.

Fields of corn were infested with cocklebur, a weed with small oblong pods covered with sharp prickly tines that stick to clothing and animal hair much like Velcro fasteners stick together. (Cockleburs were in fact the inspiration for the inventor of Velcro.) "Cockleburs are wicked, like an invention of the devil," Mama Jane was known to say. "They were second in wickedness to stinging worms. Those fat green worms with the prickly poison stingers on their backs. Stinging worms were the same color as cotton leaves and left a large swollen itchy patch wherever they touched a person's body. Such things were much harder on women folk than on men folk. In those days, women folk couldn't wear the pants and heavy work shirts like they do today. It just wasn't allowed; especially in the South."

It was always hard, if not impossible, for black families to end the year with a monetary balance. "Only a few renters like ourselves ever realized any cash returns for their labors," our aunt told us. "Plantation families were, and still are, furnished with food and the means of making the annual crop from the 'company store.' This 'store' belonged to the plantation owner, who set all prices and kept all records of a family's purchases, and so could decide what a family's income should be. At the end of the season, seems like they were always told that they had been provided much more than they had made from their crop; that they owed the plantation owner money. The sharecroppers were continuously in debt to the owners and could not leave the plantations. Often plantation sharecroppers had to fight their way off the plantation or steal away in the night and just disappear to get free.

"Good farm workers were often at a premium after the end of slavery, when many blacks left the South whenever possible for places that offered more opportunities and less tribulations. So when plantation owners found good workers they would even resort to holding them on the plantations against their will. One cousin's family, the Duckworths, had to move their meager belongings from one plantation over a period of weeks before they could steal away in the middle of the night. The owners of the plantation they left looked for them for months because they said the 'Ducks' were the best workers they had found since the War ended. Had they been found, an attempt would have been made to return them to the plantation, even at the threat of death.

"Papa, a renter living on my uncle Perry's place, sometimes cleared as much as $125 a year when I was a young girl in the 1870s. Such years, though few and far between, brought a bit of relief from the usual subsistence provided by what the family could raise, sew, or otherwise provide for themselves. There might even be an occasional peppermint stick and surprises at Christmastime," Mama Jane told us.

"Those were hard times for everybody," Mama Jane often said, "and young people were desperate to find any way to better their condition. There was hardly ever any money cleared from backbreaking year-round work. The meager subsistence was obtained from the garden or livestock raised by the family, although some plantations' owners refused to allow space for gardens or livestock. This, of course, kept the families dependent on the owners. Marriage, though often disastrous, especially for the woman, seemed the answer all too often to the miserable plantation conditions. More often than not, marriage meant just leaving one plantation for another," observed Mama Jane. "Especially when the man fell into the same trap as his father because of a lack of education and training. Often the women then just accepted their condition passively. There was no advantage in returning home and divorce was almost unheard of, and besides, there was usually no money to obtain one."

Mama Jane married William (Buddy Will) Jordan when she was seventeen or eighteen years old. From what we have learned about her younger years, we can well imagine what this twenty-seven-year-old man saw in her. For one thing, she had beauty: about five feet, five inches tall, a slim 112 pounds, with long black hair and medium dark complexion. She had high cheekbones and slightly round-faced features to catch a gentleman's fancy. We were told she had the fire and enthusiasm of a young thoroughbred.

The family also liked Buddy Will. He was a railroad man with a good steady job and lived in the much larger town of Greenwood, about twenty-five miles north of Tchula. And he had a car! According to Mama Jane, she was in seventh heaven. Buddy Will was a dashing, older

A Mississippi Album

"Grandmother Catherine" (Catherine Archer), date unknown
(Archer Family Archives)

Market day in Lexington, near the courthouse, 1930s *(Mississippi Department of Archives and History)*

Papa (Chalmers Archer, Sr.) in U.S. Artillery uniform during World War I, Paris, France *(Archer Family Archives)*

Left to right: Chalmers Archer, Jr., Hermione Archer, and Francis Archer, 1930s *(Archer Family Archives)*

Papa and his five youngest children, 1947 (Archer Family Archives)

Papa in the 1930s
(Archer Family
Archives)

The Archer children, about 1948 *(Archer Family Archives)*

Chalmers Archer, Jr., about nine months old *(Archer Family Archives)*

Aunt Statia Benjamin, about 1938 *(Archer Family Archives)*

Mama (Eva Rutherford Archer) at age sixteen *(Archer Family Archives)*

Lexington, about 1940 *(Mississippi Department of Archives and History)*

A street scene in Holmes County, 1930s *(Mississippi Department of Archives and History)*

Grandfather Payton
and a granddaugh-
ter, date unknown
*(Archer Family
Archives)*

"Uncle Nick" (Nick Archer), about
1950 *(Archer Family Archives)*

"Mama Lucy" (Lucy Parham), Eva Archer's mother, about 1950 *(Archer Family Archives)*

Aunt Statia Benjamin, about 1938 *(Archer Family Archives)*

Noonday break from cotton chopping, early 1950s *(Archer Family Archives)*

Uncle Joseph (husband of Aunt Fannie) plowing, 1940s *(Archer Family Archives)*

Holmes County Courthouse, about 1929 *(Office of the Chancery Clerk, Lexington, Mississippi)*

Saints Industrial and Literary School, where Eva Archer taught, 1940s *(Mississippi Department of Archives and History)*

School near Tchula, Mississippi, 1930s *(Mississippi Department of Archives and History)*

A street scene in Holmes County, 1930s *(Mississippi Department of Archives and History)*

man. By any criteria, a very good catch: a man she and the family liked and an escape from the farm's backbreaking work!

By the time the younger generation came to know her, Mama Jane was the reigning matriarch of the family. Her black heritage was passed on to us through the stories she told about how the family had lived and was married to the land. We could readily see and understand her primal ethic in the way she focused on making life better for herself and the family. Nevertheless, Mama Jane was a complex individual with conflicting personal ideologies.

There were vivid contradictions in her thought and nature. Whereas she often talked of the importance of being black and bettering oneself as a black person, she herself accepted or rejected people because of the color of their skin. Her thinking in this area was diametrically opposed to that of the rest of the family.

Buddy Will and Mama Jane became the parents of two children: Willie Payton, the "black one," and Doll Baby, the "white one." Doll Baby was accepted by her mother, but Willie Payton never was. Early in life, Willie Payton was sent from his parents' home to live with various relatives because of the color of his skin.

Although most of the time Mama Jane was an agreeably pleasant person, at times she would be acerbic, temperamental, and obstinate. In all her ninety-nine years, even in later years, no one could change her mind on the skin color matter. Mama Jane could or never would admit that her position on skin color constituted a belief in white racial superiority. "Her relatives all tried hard, to no avail, to come to a conclusion as to why she thought as she did," one of her siblings told me.

Reconstruction was a key element of her mind-set, in addition to her particular family heritage. During Mama Jane's early years she was influenced by whites who worked hard to convince black people that they were inherently inferior to whites. According to the version of American history that she learned, whites had effected everything worthwhile that had been achieved in the young country, especially in the South. Newly freed slaves were taught the status quo had to be preserved to protect the southern traditions and civilization. The only conclusion the family could come to was that because Mama Jane was born and grew up so soon after the Civil War, she was brainwashed by the events of the time. Mama Jane told us quite sincerely one day, "White people taught us well. We came to know that we should help keep black and white people from mixing on social levels and prevent intermarriage between the races."

Whereas my generation—and even Mama Jane's younger brothers and sisters—contended that traditional values and beliefs prevalently held by whites were abhorrent, she differed with us. On the other hand, she often said that many whites were not in full agreement with the idea of white superiority but dared not say so.

She cited the teachings of white preachers among her chief reasons for supporting her points of view on color, intermarriage, and social "mixing." It seems she accepted their views on religion; their teachings included admonitions that the Bible said slaves should obey their masters.

Ironically, Mama Jane appeared to realize the terrible hardships that most blacks had to bear. She spoke eloquently about the rigid segregation during Reconstruction and its aftermath, in housing, transportation, education, and places of amusement. To enforce the segregation laws, violators were threatened with death. "We children," she would confess to us, "were treated just like a little dog or monkey. It amused the white people to pet or kick us as they pleased."

Nevertheless, in the next breath, Mama Jane would tell us how her parents told her about church services on the plantation during slavery. "There was a church on the plantation and both white and black people went there together for Sunday school and preaching service. We were told to serve and be true to 'our God.' The preacher would also tell us we must obey our missus and master. He told us that we must be obedient to them. That is what he told us, all right," Mama Jane quoted her mother, Catherine, as saying.

"I remember so well the very seat where I sat in the white people's church. Each Sunday my black and white family sat bathed in the soft, filtered blue light, made by the sun coming through the stained glass behind us. This was wonderful," Mama Jane's mother told her.

Mama Jane's stories helped reinforce our sense of history and purpose. Frankly, with Mama Jane around we could not forget who we were. Many of her tales were almost classroom lectures, but they were still important to us all. The whole community, especially the family, wanted to hear this unbroken black history, in all its spectrum of colors.

Our aunt, as far as we can tell, was the great, great, great, great granddaughter of a slave who arrived at a Mississippi bottoms plantation in a covered wagon near Greenwood about two hundred years ago.

"We did not experience overt racism for a while after freedom," she was told by her parents. "There were, until Reconstruction, no 'colored only' facilities like segregated waiting rooms. We all sat together." Mama Jane seemed to think sitting together was special, unique. We kids always thought, but kept to ourselves, that blacks sat with and went everywhere whites did during slavery too. But they were not really together. They were not free. Still, these tales to us were real stories of the days when shackles were cast off black people. These times, we were sure, were the first gleanings of hope for the newly freed slaves like her parents.

Mama Jane's stories really brought to life the South of the late 1800s. During our generation of the 1950s and 1960s, learning and understanding this history was often difficult. But it was made easier from the way our aunt told about it. She made what, at the time, was a recent but important piece of black history come to life.

She also helped us appreciate and experience the world, nature and the seasons, swamps and bayous. She gave us a sense of place: farms and fields, hills to the east, the great river to the west. Her nature tales were frequently interspersed with stories of many murdered black men and women; murdered by white vigilantes, their bodies thrown in the swamps and bayous around Greenwood during her early years.

"I remember," Mama Jane would often say, "during or shortly after Reconstruction, how the whitecappers [the Klan] whipped and scared us during the nights." These whitecappers were vigilante groups committed to lynch-law methods to drive away, coerce, or kill blacks who did not conform to their ideas of white superiority. "It was that terrible vigilantism," she would say. One time she showed us whips, shackles, and stocks used during slavery that one relative had held on to for many years.

Mama Jane would often jump from the horrors of slavery to the country wisdom her parents learned from necessity during this period. She would demonstrate how to chew small branches of certain trees until they become pliant, then explain how to dip them in a mixture of baking soda and salt to brush one's teeth. She could go from the simple practicalities of farm life to detailed lessons on looms and weaving.

Our aunt was also an authority on ghosts and the supernatural. "Yes, ghosts are presences that can't always be seen as something terrible," she would say. She liked to tell about the time she lived in the domestic servants' cabin on one plantation called Pinchback. "Upon arrival at Pinchback, I felt a presence looming over me and heard my name called when no one was present but me." This "presence" never harmed her but she knew it was there. Furthermore, she knew many people who could provide one with a "hand"; a good-luck charm that would ward off bad luck. "There were also plenty of people who could remove a spell from the 'conjured' or 'conjure' anyone who you didn't like and wanted to harm; even remove a snake from those who had been hexed. Some of these conjurers were family members," she would say with a laugh.

Hexes and good-luck "hands" worked because of an individual's belief in them. One can be hexed by merely sprinkling plain self-rising flour, baby powder, or talcum powder around any place the person may be. The belief of the subject being hexed is the main ingredient in this action. (I know this to be true because I once tried to put a hex on a gullible person and almost scared him to death with only the rudimentary knowledge that I have about conjuring. This individual was scared and angry enough with me to do me serious bodily harm.)

At times hexes can include miniature lifelike dolls that contain various things from an individual's body such as cut fingernails and hair. Individuals who believe in such things think that damage to these dolls will cause them corresponding pain. Good-luck "hands" operate in a similar manner. If an individual believes, any number or manner of things can be used in these amulets.

The snakes were mostly "removed" from the subject in one or two ways. One way was to induce the subject to vomit with an emetic such as ipecac. Then botfly or other such eggs would be placed in this solution, and the subject would be told to wait for a day or two. When the eggs hatched into larvae, the subject would be sure they were young snakes that would continue to grow. The advantage to this method was the subject would think that the individual who had removed the "snake or snakes" had caused them to appear as if by magic, in the same manner as the conjurer had placed them inside him or her.

Another method of removing snakes or other vermin from a subject was through sleight of hand. As we all know, the hand is quicker than the eye. So after the subject had been induced to vomit, small snakes would be placed in the vomit to cause wonderment in the subject. Having faith in the "doctor" would effect a psychological improvement in the subject's condition.

Often I have thought that Mama Jane considered herself something of a conjurer. She had a cure for everything that afflicts humankind. Some of these cures, she said, were hundreds of years old. They were handed down from Grandma Catherine's grandmother's era and eventually on down to her.

Whether some of her remedies worked to one's benefit or detriment was a matter of opinion. These cures included taking dried cow chips and corn shucks, boiling them, and drinking this boiled liquid as hot as possible to cure the common cold. Shuck tea, without the cow chips, has in fact long been used as a means to "bring out the bumps" in measles. Papa said this is a tried-and-true remedy.

At one time Papa had a place on his leg that itched terribly, and his incessant scratching was beginning to form an ulcerlike sore. Mama Jane told him to take the leaves of the jimson weed, a poisonous annual weed of the nightshade family, which usually grows in the fertile soil around barns, and wrap them around his leg tightly with gauze. This, she told him, would cure his leg where the doctor's efforts had failed. The remedy proved successful, albeit painful. Papa said, "Never before had anything been so painful except one bad toothache I had as a young adult." He never had any further trouble from this leg itch.

Another of Mama Jane's remedies was the drinking of horse's milk. This milk was usually given to children who had difficulties in teething.

Mama said this remedy was tried out on me at Mama Jane's insistence, because I cried so while teething.

As Mama Jane told us, Grandpa Payton and Grandma Catherine frequently explained to her that black people experienced much less overt racism right after slavery ended. "It was," they explained, "as if white people were trying to make up for the wrongs they had inflicted on us during the two hundred and forty-six years of slavery."

"Not that all white people of that era were kind and benevolent to black people," Mama Jane took great pains to explain. "There were always bands of marauding renegade whites who attacked black families without reason and many innocent people were killed." Mama Jane said they seemed to want to take out their frustrations of having lost the War on black people.

Everybody has heard stories about Quantrill's Raiders rampaging and killing across the country for the Confederacy during the War. Of course they killed whites as well as blacks who were not in sympathy with the Southern cause. Whereas Quantrill's Raiders became famous nationwide, there were many smaller groups that never made the headlines.

"Grandma Catherine had two theories as to why whites were so nice and passive toward blacks right after the Civil War ended," Mama Jane said. "First of all, and most important, there was a definite fear by whites that the federal troops might intervene if they became too violent toward blacks. But more likely, many whites who had once been rich, powerful plantation owners found themselves pauper poor like the newly freed slaves. Homes were burned and crops ruined or not harvested when blacks could not or would not work for their 'masters' near the end of the war.

"A lot of whites hired their former slaves for just the food they could eat. Other blacks became sharecroppers for other whites, because field work was all they had ever known and did not have the spine to try anything on their own. These sharecroppers would have to give the landowner most of what they produced. Mama [Catherine] said many of the house blacks who thought they had been well treated by their white owners even fought other blacks who urged them to make a break from their white folks.

"Black men were able to vote and had all the civil rights that whites had right after the War, Mama told us children. At first the federal troops ensured that we had these rights and many blacks became important people like Mississippi state and United States senators and other politicians. Black folk held every kind of job. For example, my sister Statia's husband, Mr. Cal, had the general store and was a mail rider for years. This state of affairs went on for many years until many of these jobs were taken from black folks by the night riders, the state legislature, and the courts."

Mama Jane said the night riders killed, and burned down the houses of many, many black people soon after the War. "Most black folks had no way to protect themselves but, more often than not, they fought these marauders in any way they could. But they always had less firepower and were outnumbered. These cowards in large groups attacked small numbers of blacks."

I can remember Papa telling us about the time when he was about eleven years old and encountered nearly one hundred Ku Klux Klansmen, all riding mules draped in white.

"These Klansmen were all wearing white robes and pointed white hats," Papa said. "I ran and hid under a bridge. It seemed hours before I heard the last of the mules crossing that bridge. After they were out of sight, I ran all the way home."

Papa said he never found out why these Klansmen were riding about on a public road that day. Grandpa Payton told him they were probably out riding just to make an impression on black people to ensure they knew and kept their places. Papa recalled, "Grandpa Payton said to just forget them. That they were really cowards and depended on large groups such as that to frighten folks. Although they were, Grandpa emphasized, very dangerous. They used such numbers to beat and even lynch individuals or small groups of blacks. Even entire families."

Mama Jane declared, "After years of seeing and hearing about their family members beaten and even killed by such men during slavery and after slavery, it is easy to see how such groups were very scary to black folks. Many kids your father's age did not have a Grandpa Payton with the wisdom to quell their fears, even though they were probably as apprehensive as your father was. These groups were indeed danger-ous!"

Mama Jane told us that segregation "came about because law enforcement and the courts did not act to stop such groups as these. Black folks were completely cowed. And when these white racists got the upper hand in the state and passed Jim Crow laws, the courts did nothing to stop them or overturn the laws." I recall the bitterness in her voice, the resignation.

"Even when black people were elected to local or state offices, they were prevented from doing their jobs by these same types of white racists. And the courts allowed it when the all-white legislature passed laws that said it was all right to set up separate facilities for blacks.

"The coming of the night riders changed, for the next hundred years, the accommodating conditions for blacks in the South," Mama Jane said Grandma Catherine had told her. "As I said, the sight and actions of these night riders frightened many blacks into not fighting back when the state legislatures passed laws that said blacks could not go where whites did not want them. I can remember when many of these laws were passed.

"These laws said in a nicer way the same thing that slavery's [Dred] Scott decision said. Blacks were not citizens and had few rights. As you know, these separate but equal laws were not changed until just a few years ago after being passed many, many years ago." And Mama Jane insisted that "the Klan night riders are the same today as they were during and right after slavery."

Her mother had told her that she, Catherine, had not been treated as badly as Grandpa Payton during slavery. Catherine had been related to her owners, who had admitted the relationship, so she had been given less harsh treatment than most of the plantation's slaves. Mama Jane said, "My mother, your Grandma Catherine, was treated kindly as one would treat a favorite hunting dog." Even so, her situation was not the norm. Most women, related to their owners or not, were treated the same as beasts of burden during slavery.

"So," Mama Jane said, "This was no honor. Anyone's life as a slave is almost impossible to imagine. For someone else to have total control over your destiny is a continuous nightmare from which you never awaken unless freed. Your Grandpa's life, though, until the end of slavery was much more hellish."

Grandma Catherine said the separation of her family during slavery constituted more than inhuman treatment. Many members of her family were never seen or heard from again after being sold to different plantation owners. Close members of her family were simply put on the auction block, bought by strangers, and led away, sometimes in chains, no matter what manner of importuning was tried by those left behind. "It did not matter whether you were related to the plantation owner by blood or not," Mama Jane quoted Grandma Catherine as often saying. "You were not considered human and treated like cattle if you had *any* Negro blood.

"Your Grandpa Payton was also separated from his family by sale, but in his case, he was the one sold away from his family," Mama Jane quoted Grandma Catherine as saying. "His life consisted only of beating and work. A short while after being bought at about eleven years old your grandpa was given an initiation into his new home with a cruel beating by his new master. He always regretted he never tried to escape even at his young age. From right before the War until the end of the War, Grandpa Payton said he saw many slaves shot, hanged, or literally beaten to death for attempts to escape. He could only blame his youth for his inaction."

Grandpa Payton never found many close members of his family after the War, eventually finding only one sister. But Grandma Catherine found her brother Perry and other family members. "Your granduncle Perry was quite an interesting character," Mama Jane told us kids. "Right after the War he just fenced in approximately five hundred acres out near Mount Olive, paid taxes on it, and declared it was his. He kept this land for nearly forty-five years and passed it on to his son. Nevertheless this son did not keep the land for very long. Something of a ne'er-do-well all his life, he immediately proceeded to gamble it away. He lost the whole place through his gambling." Again, I hear the bitterness in her voice. But also the spunk.

Grandpa Payton and Grandma Catherine rented land from her brother Perry for many years before he died and the land was lost.

They are buried either on the old Perry land or very near it. But it was only after Papa's death that we realized that nobody but he knew the exact boundaries of the land or even where our grandparents are buried.

Papa had taken us out to where Grandpa Payton, Grandma Catherine, and various other relatives are buried and found that several small trees had grown near the graves. Later, when Papa said that he would cut these trees, Mama Jane had said excitedly, "Chat, if those trees are cut you will destroy the souls of our parents and bring yourself a lifetime of bad luck!" She always called him Chat, especially when she was agitated. So Papa did not cut the trees and we never went back to the burial place, which disappeared as the trees took over. Mama Jane had added one more bit of old folklore, which had been handed down from generation to generation, to our family memories.

8 Tales of Birth and Death

Time has not eroded my vivid memories of the little shanties, usually situated several yards from the only slightly larger houses in many black neighborhoods during the 1930s and 1940s. These shanties were one-room constructions and usually crudely built. So crudely constructed, in fact, that one would think that they would have served better as storage sheds than living quarters for sick people.

These cabins were symptomatic and symbolic of the health conditions that black people had to contend with during much of this century. Specifically, the shanties were the "outhouses" where people who suffered from tuberculosis had to live to prevent their passing the disease to the rest of their families. Diseases like tuberculosis were much more prevalent among blacks than whites because the conditions under which they lived were more conducive to getting such diseases.

Today, of course, tuberculosis is not usually the debilitating disease it once was. But before the advent of modern medicine, tuberculosis was a dreaded nemesis, and if it was even suspected, the individual had to be totally isolated.

This isolation meant living in the one-room shack, sometimes for many years. The individual could seldom leave, and no one else could enter. Food and the other necessities of life had to be passed in and out. Anything that came from inside these probably infested living quarters had to be sterilized by scalding or destroyed by burning. Many blacks ended their days in the infamous TB shanties.

Some members of our family have always contended that Mama Jane's daughter, Doll Baby, died at a very young age as a result of having had tuberculosis. Nevertheless, she was not kept in an "outhouse." Mama Jane always kept her in the house with her, and nobody else in the family became infected.

Doll Baby was credited with being a very beautiful child, acceptable in looks to please Mama Jane. Unlike her son, Willie Payton, for whom she showed almost no affection, Doll Baby was always the apple of her mother's eye and dressed in the finest clothes of the era with no regard for cost. Indulged in every way, Doll Baby was not allowed to play with any other children and was kept indoors at all times.

In fact, one of our aunts claimed that Doll Baby was not allowed to play at all. "She was forced to sit elegantly dressed from morning to night with only her dolls as companions. She did not get enough exercise and fresh air and was likely to fall prey to any number of deadly diseases." No medical doctor ever determined a definite cause for her early death.

In fact, many illnesses and deaths of blacks remained a mystery. Unless people exhibited classic symptoms, nobody knew for sure what disease they really had. This fact makes statistics on black deaths suspect for that era. Also, Mississippi elects its local county coroners through popular elections, and this means every death certificate for people who die outside of hospital care is suspect. County coroners can be elected even if they have only a high school diploma.

Housing for blacks, on and off the plantations, was in disreputable condition. Housing was almost always insufficient for the size of the family required to live in it. Even in the 1940s, houses in rural areas were chronically without screens and necessary toilet facilities; many did not even have outdoor toilet facilities. Therefore, conditions were rife for the spread of diseases caused by flies, mosquitoes, rats, and even those diseases passed from person to person.

Further, blacks were much less aware than whites of the conditions that would give rise to diseases such as polio, smallpox, and yellow fever. Compounding this problem was the fact some uneducated blacks believed that all illnesses were acts of God rained down on them as punishment for their sins or those of their fathers, and so they made no attempt to protect themselves even in ways open to them.

Nonetheless, many blacks took precautions against such diseases as polio, one of the scourges of the 1930s and 1940s. Crowds were to be avoided, since polio was thought to be more communicable in crowded places, especially in warm weather. I remember Mama and Papa warning us repeatedly not to swim in large groups in the blue holes of the creeks that flowed near our home in Lexington, especially during the dog days of summer or extremely hot weather. These blue holes— deep pools found naturally in the creeks—were perfect for swimming and drew kids from all around the town. Despite the polio scares, the swimming holes were a magnet for the young in July and August. Mama would also use atomizers to spray the throats of neighborhood children with quinine and other mixtures obtained from a local doctor to ward off polio during summer months. Of course, although none of these remedies were really effective prevention, few in our surrounding area got polio.

Papa said there were epidemics in the state that took untold numbers of lives of blacks because of their lack of proper health care and living conditions. "I know," Papa said, "that Grandma Catherine died in the influenza epidemic because she just did not have adequate medical help. Professional medical treatment was almost unheard of for anything but the most severe illnesses and, in cases like this flu epidemic, blacks were totally disregarded."

Whenever anyone "had the doctor," you could be sure that person was desperately ill. Blacks were reluctant to seek medical help for two reasons. First, they lacked the money—even though, as my father recalled, "a visit to the doctor cost fifty cents to one dollar." Second, white physicians frequently did not want to treat black patients and showed it through their demeanor. This attitude caused many blacks to avoid doctors until their conditions were medically hopeless.

These were the days before Medicaid and even before farmers were protected under the social security system. "If a family did not have ready cash or something with which to barter, they were usually denied medical treatment," Papa said.

Although some doctors would not treat blacks, luckily, during most of the 1930s and for two more decades Holmes County had one white physician who was a friend to all, black and white alike. He was an excellent "country" doctor who never turned away anyone from his door, but even he could not treat everybody. The days were too short, and the Delta too large. This physician was a recent immigrant; he did not exhibit the prejudices common to local whites. His office was frequently full. So, out of necessity, blacks developed their own cure-alls for most of the illnesses that afflicted them.

For sure, there was no true therapeutic value in many of the folk remedies and practices used by many people, but perhaps some of them did work because the practitioner had such faith in them. I remember as a child I had a small growth on the side of my head removed by Aunt Sally, Mama Lucy's older sister. Aunt Sally tried the following remedy on my wart, which could have proved to be a dangerous growth. First she "sterlized" a needle by heating it until it became red hot. Next, the needle was used to pick at the wart until it bled. A piece of bread was then soaked in this blood and dropped over my shoulder for the chickens to eat. The wart or growth did not return.

Another remedy that I remember was the practice of measuring a child who appeared to be growing too slowly in order to stimulate his or her growth.

I happened to be a late grower and was "measured" by Aunt Statia, because some of the family believed that my growth had been stunted. The process involved measuring one's foot and body with a small string at regular intervals and uttering a special prayerlike incantation. This was done several times over a period of two or three years. I did grow finally, but not because of Aunt Statia's "measuring." Hormones and good nutrition likely did the trick. Still it was comforting to have the aid of Aunt Statia's ancient prayers, as well.

Kerosene, or coal oil as it was more commonly called, was a panacea for blacks for many, many years dating from the days of slavery. Even today many blacks place unbelievable faith in coal oil. An elderly man recently told me that he used coal oil to relieve the symptoms of gangrene due to complications from diabetes, along with the prescriptions from his doctor. I suspect he might have been using coal oil alone, rather than continuing to see his physician and follow his directions. However, it is nice to think these things sometimes do work in harmony together.

Coal oil was used to treat just about any malady afflicting black people and many whites. Because most blacks did not routinely receive tetanus shots, coal oil took the place of these shots. In a rural area like Holmes County, most blacks worked or played around barnyards or other such areas, where tetanus germs are said to abound on the rusty nails, implements, and animal manure found in these places. Whenever any of us children received a wound from stepping on a rusty nail around the barn, we were immediately told to carefully wash the area around the wound first in soapy water and then apply coal oil liberally to the wound.

Here are two more examples that show the versatility of coal oil When I had a tooth pulled by the only dentist then in the county, Mama Lucy told me to immediately rinse my mouth with "straight" coal oil to get rid of the soreness caused by the extraction. And whenever anyone displayed the first symptoms of the common cold, Papa would mix sugar and coal oil and burn them together to make homemade cough drops and a concoction to relieve chest discomfort.

Coal oil, of course, was a main source of energy for our lighting, as well as for much of the heat not coming from wool. Families not living close to the small towns did not get electricity until the late 1940s. Coal oil was a multipurpose commodity for many families.

Lack of health facilities for blacks involved every aspect of our lives, including orthodontia. Two of my brothers had at least one tooth that grew in at an odd angle. Mama took the two of them at an early age to the only dentist in Lexington to inquire about the possibility and effectiveness of braces in both their cases.

Mama said, "The dentist did not even look at the condition of either child's teeth. He just immediately went into an angry harangue about my inability to pay for braces for one child's teeth, let alone braces for two children's teeth. No matter how many times I tried to ask him how much the braces would be, he just continued the diatribe about how I couldn't pay for braces.

"I never learned if the dentist didn't want any black child to be seen with braces, or if he just didn't know how to use braces to correct dental problems. No matter how I tried to broach the question of cost and effectiveness of braces, the dentist wouldn't budge from his position that I couldn't pay for braces for even one child. White children in the county had long been seen with braces. I have always thought that his apparent anger just meant that a black person shouldn't have had the audacity to ask a white doctor for braces, to think they needed them, or even to want them." As it turned out, neither brother ever got braces and, alas, both grew up with crooked teeth.

Then there were those aspects of life that unhappily involved the insect world. Chinches or bedbugs were the scourge of one's life in the cramped living quarters of most blacks. Chinches infested people's homes, especially their beds, and would crawl out at night, feasting on the blood of everyone from the youngest to the oldest. They would also contaminate the family's clothing and furniture. Many times chinches or bedbugs could be seen crawling on people in public. They could hide in the tiniest places and appear at the most embarrassing times.

At first chinches, fleas, flies, mosquitoes, and other insect pests were controlled as best one could by putting coal oil on bed linens and even on one's person. Various solutions were concocted to protect all of us from the incessant biting gnats, flies, and mosquitoes ubiquitous to the Delta. These biting and disease-carrying insects were much worse on the Place near the low-lying Delta than on our farm near Lexington. Mama Jane, Aunt Statia, Uncle Perry, and Uncle Nick would argue about what was the best type of wood to use in the evening "smokes" to ward off biting pests.

Often people would build fires to create a smoke that was thought to be noxious to mosquitoes and other flying insect pests. Different kinds of woods were used, and at times greenery from some plants would be put atop the burning wood to create extra smoke. I have always thought it was the smoke alone that drove away the black gnats and mosquitoes and not the type of wood or greenery used. Whereas I cannot now remember what specific woods we had to gather for the "smokes," I do remember that none seemed to work better than others.

There was no known way to rid one's home of chinches until the formulation of the insecticide dichloro-diphenyl-trichloro-ethane, commonly known as DDT. At the time, however, DDT seemed a miraculous cure: it all but eradicated chinches and other household pests. In the middle 1940s, county health department sprayers went from house to house all over the county to spray them with DDT. Beddings, clothing, and other household furnishings were sprayed directly with the potent insecticide. It was also used as a means of eradicating mosquitoes in low-lying areas that were known to harbor mosquito-bearing stagnant water.

DDT proved to be an extremely effective insecticide. Nevertheless, as everybody now knows, it proved to have some very serious side effects and caused many problems with increases in the rodent and snake populations. This occurred when DDT found its way into surface and ground water, and fish, frogs, and other food for birds of prey became infested with DDT. When these were eaten by the birds of prey, the DDT caused the shells of their eggs to become too soft to support the unhatched bird embryos. Consequently, these birds almost became extinct. The populations of rodents and snakes increased, as the numbers of their "hawkish" predators decreased.

This effect from widespread use of DDT in the late 1940s and early 1950s has been proved. But no one can be sure what the result will be on the people who also ate, slept, and generally lived with DDT that was sprayed in their homes every spring for five or six years. The all-white health department workers who sprayed our homes would spray every nook and cranny, including the kitchens and beds. Afterward, they would proudly tack a small placard on the front of the house that stated when the house had been sprayed. Once when I asked if everybody's homes were being treated, they answered, "Boy, your people are calling us blessed. We are cleaning up these places." This statement, I always believed, meant the homes of black people.

DDT may still be having an unhealthy effect on us. The fact is, just the runoff from DDT in the food chain of birds of prey caused genetic mutations in their reproductive cycles. And this potent insecticide was sprayed directly in the living areas of people's homes all across the state.

<center>~~~~~~~</center>

The birth of a neighbor's child provided high drama for my younger sister, brother, and me. Births and deaths were always close at hand. On this occasion, the neighbor lived about two miles from the Place. The flushed and feverish mother was about to give birth to her sixth child and showed signs of being seriously ill. It was a difficult labor. We kids received the news in anxious installments. It was another adventure with Papa as the hero.

A local doctor came to stay only long enough to inform the family that neither mother nor child would probably survive. The woman's husband asked the physician, "What do you think we should do, doctor?" "Probably get her to the hospital as fast as you can," the doctor advised. "There is nothing that I can do for her here. But you had better see to it that she does not get chilled or exposed because she probably has double pneumonia already."

Because neither Papa nor that family had a car at the time, the worried husband asked the doctor what would be the effect of his taking his wife to the nearest hospital in Lexington some eight miles away in a mule-drawn wagon, his only means of transportation. "She might not last the trip, and the baby probably will die too," the doctor replied. The distraught man then asked if the doctor could use his own car to transport the suffering woman to the hospital. The physician did not even respond to the suggestion. He ignored it, and simply said, "You get your wife to the hospital, and I will do what I can for her there, when I see her tomorrow." He then left.

Not knowing anything else to do, but disregarding the doctor's ominous prediction, Papa and the worried husband began several frantic days of around-the-clock work on the mother and her new baby, who was safely, miraculously delivered. The two men pressed herbal poultices onto the mother's strangely blotched skin and forced her to drink herbal toddies that Mama said had worked on her patients before. They pulled thick blobs of mucus from the new baby's throat, often while holding her upside down by her ankles. Sometimes they even forced her to cry to help clear her lungs and throat.

Nobody ever found out if the mother really suffered from double pneumonia. The baby girl's malady was similarly of an unknown nature, but she and her mother survived.

Many such events seemed miracles indeed for black people who had no recourse but to provide their own medical relief, because professional help was unavailable, inaccessible, or indifferent. Nevertheless, some cases required professional aid despite the heroic efforts of family and friends.

My younger brother developed what we believe was pneumonia after his birth at home in Lexington. Soon after he was born, my brother began to have trouble breathing and acquired a yellowish tinge to his skin that Mama, Papa, the midwife, and various relatives called yellow jaundice. As a youngster, I remember I had no idea what yellow jaundice meant, but the adults all seemed to think this condition was much worse than the breathing difficulty. I could imagine having a brother tinged by a curious "yellowness" that would embarrass the family by his looking different from everybody else. To me, it really had no serious health effect. The kid was just turning yellow. But, of course, it did.

The midwife was obviously seriously worried. She told Papa, "The baby needs to go to the hospital, but to get him there will cause him to be exposed to the cold, wet [December] weather. His only hope is for us to get a doctor out here as soon as possible." Having no telephone, Papa set out to find the only doctor in Lexington.

Because he could not find the doctor immediately, Papa was gone for almost the entire day. During his absence, neighbors came and went, each giving advice on what should be done to save the sick baby. But, because the newborn would not breast-feed and would take only a few sips of milk from a bottle, the only thing that could be done for him was to apply a mustard plaster and wrap him in warm woolen blankets.

Mustard plasters were flannel cloths impregnated with various things that included dry mustard, Vicks salve, turpentine, camphor, coal oil, and other concoctions; they were placed on the chest to cure common colds and other chest ailments. Each person who visited that day seemed to recommend different things to be used in the preparation of the mustard plaster. Uncle Nick was a confirmed believer in the use of mustard plasters and left explicit instructions before he left to help Papa find the doctor.

With the baby seemingly sinking beyond anyone's ability to help him, he was placed on the bed wrapped in his flannel mustard plaster and woolen blanket. The bedroom, heated by a roaring fire in the fireplace, seemed overly hot to me, even in the cold December weather. Mama and some neighbors sat in a dispirited semicircle around the fireplace, and I watched to see just how yellow the baby would become.

Papa, who had left the house hours earlier, had wanted Uncle Nick with him because Uncle Nick was more aggressive when aroused than Papa by nature could ever be. Visiting the doctor's office every thirty minutes, Papa was told the doctor was not in but not where he might be reached.

Papa said later, "I walked the town square of Lexington until I thought that my toes, nose, and fingers would drop off from the cold. I'll bet I walked twenty miles from Shaddock and Kimbrough grocery store to the dry goods store on the opposite corner of the square where I could see the doctor's office and the rest of Court Square.

"Finally my patience was rewarded when I spotted the doctor leaving one of the dry goods stores on the square. When I approached him and explained the situation, he demurred; he obviously did not want to make a late afternoon home visit. The doctor, with a fierce frown, said he had other patients to see that afternoon, but changed his mind when I told him he had to come, and right then."

Papa explained that the doctor said he changed his mind when he decided he could test this new medicine he called penicillin on a patient who possibly had pneumonia. "I didn't care at that point why he was coming; I just knew he had to come and I think that he knew I was determined that he would come. I appreciated the ride home in his new car but the trip seemed interminably long."

My younger brother survived, we still believe, because of the effectiveness of the medicine the doctor gave him late that December day. Although in his younger days he suffered from asthma (which he ultimately outgrew in his teen years), he suffered no long-range effects from the illness in his infancy. But we could never determine if the medicine the doctor used was really penicillin. If it was penicillin, my brother must have been one of the first patients to whom it was given.

An even younger brother was stillborn, even though Mama had been hospitalized before his birth. Everybody said that he died because Mama ate some fresh meat a few days before his birth. Aunt Mary, Uncle Nick's wife, sent word that Mama should not eat any of the opossum that some hunter had given Papa the day before, since this would be bad for the expected baby. The warning came too late, for Mama had tasted the meat the previous day. Ironically, this was the first and last time she had eaten opossum. Whereas neither Mama nor Papa believed fresh meat, even opossum, could have had anything to do with the fact that the baby was stillborn, Aunt Mary and assorted other relatives always contended it was the cause of the baby's not surviving.

One of my first cousins died in childbirth, due to what was called a breech birth, in the early 1950s. Living far out in a rural area, the mother could not get to a doctor in time, nor get one to come to her home. When she finally did get to the closest hospital, about nine or ten miles from her home, nothing could be done. Several relatives came to give blood the hospital said she needed, or offer any other assistance, but it was too late.

Indifference on the part of most white physicians continued to be a major problem. There were only two or three doctors that most black people could trust or depend on in any way in the 1930s and 1940s. These were black doctors in neighboring counties, an extremely rare commodity anywhere in Mississippi in those days. When things became desperate medically, people would first make every effort to contract one of these doctors. In one of his books, a well-known white novelist from the area has credited one of these black doctors with saving his life. Limited finances often prohibited all but the most well-to-do blacks from being able to get to these doctors.

Strangely, according to what Mama Jane said she learned from Grandma Catherine, black people found that medical treatment was worse after slavery than during slavery. Grandma Catherine told Mama Jane, "During slavery blacks were immediately taken to the slave 'infirmary' at the first sign of malaria, yellow fever, or any deadly and contagious disease." According to Grandma Catherine, these infirmaries had medicines such as quinine, healing powders, and spirits that were kept under lock and key.

Grandma Catherine said she knew slaves received fairly good medical care because of their economic value to their masters. "Slaves," she said, "would be ruthlessly killed for certain infractions of the rules their masters thought to be dangerous to their families, or their way of life. But they realized the survival of the slaves represented the continuation of their way of life, since that depended solely on the slave's production of king cotton."

After slavery the economic value of blacks was much less, and whites were not seriously interested in their health. "Our lives were held cheaply, as there were always more cheap black laborers to be found," Papa quoted Grandma Catherine as saying. During the influenza epidemic of the early 1900s, thousands upon thousands of blacks died because of inadequate health care. Papa said the number of deaths from influenza of young and old people who otherwise seemed healthy was unbelievable; Grandma Catherine was among the victims.

"Every family within our area lost from one to three members during this epidemic. White families were struck down too," Papa said. "Hospitals were filled with whites, and doctors had little or no time for blacks. Only the knowledge gained through years of practice of folk medicine kept the death rate for blacks from going higher."

Folk medicine, I will always believe, has probably saved the lives of countless black people who did not have access to more modern medical services.

Mama and Papa always contended that black people had a lower incidence of cancer and heart disease than whites because of the types of food that they ate. Grandma Catherine and Summa, my great-grandmother, often said that during slavery, black folks got to eat the "liquor" from the vegetables that were cooked for white folks or from the few vegetables they were able to raise or otherwise gather from one source or the other. This "liquor," they contended, was the most nutritious part of food, containing most of the vitamins and minerals.

But Papa always said, "Even if the foods that blacks ate were not conducive to certain cancers, the diet was not nutritionally complete. Most blacks could not afford a variety of foods. They ate beans, peas, and the cheaper cuts of pork, sow's belly and the like."

Whenever possible, blacks raised their own hogs even when there was no room to raise vegetables or beef. These hogs usually had a high amount of fat which was rendered down into lard to be used in all of one's cooking.

Otherwise unusable fat from hogs was cooked in a large black pot over an open fire. The end result of this action was the lard, of course, but the cooked fat was coveted as cracklings, from which Mama Lucy made such delicious crackling bread, or just eaten as pork rinds are eaten today. (President Bush is reportedly fond of today's more "sanitized" cracklings.) Of course, the use of lard was very bad for people's health, but many people have contended that because black people were forced to work so hard physically they suffered less from such dietary indiscretions even when continued over long periods.

The fat from beef was rendered down into the tallow that Uncle Nick so prized for his mustard plasters used for chest colds. While tallow was not used as a food in any way, it was still a treasured possession since most people did not have cattle to slaughter from which to obtain tallow.

When I was growing up, in the 1930s and 1940s, there were many cases of serious illness all over Holmes County. The young as well as the old were victims. One young cousin developed rheumatic fever in junior high school after months of complaining of a sore throat. No doctor seemed to think his suffering from a sore throat for so long a time was in any way strange. He died when he was about sixteen. His case was representative of the many who died so young.

On the other hand, there were those individuals in the Lexington and Tchula area who were celebrated for being long-lived. We all heard of them often and, strangely, because of attention given to senior citizen birthday festivities rather than the deaths of babies, many people seemed to have the idea that blacks were not in dire straits in terms of health. The many who died in infancy and in their early youth were perhaps mercifully never dwelled upon. It was better to gaze fondly upon the survivors among us.

9 A Sense of Community

In those days, during the 1930s and 1940s, we thought a lot about other troubled people of the world. Like why did people stay where they were? Why did the Jews stay in Germany? Why did black people stay in Mississippi? In Lexington and Tchula? In America?

We believed it was because most people lived as a "community." And we in our neighborhood were attached to those around us and places around us for better or worse. Thus, many of us remained in Lexington and Tchula, in Holmes County and Mississippi. Many of us stayed because we loved the land, and many did not join the migration northward.

Out of very rough times emerged a very strong black community. We had a spirit that transformed into hopes and dreams and aspirations. Neighbors came together to talk a lot. To help each other more. To share more. To pledge that we would continue to stick together. For one thing, we were beginning to realize that Lexington, Mississippi, was as much ours as anyone else's.

Many in those days lived by the kindness of friends, with some help from a few caring whites. At certain points during those times, it was necessary for the very poor to band together to buy food and prepare meals. This was usually necessary only in the towns. In these situations, a sense of community truly meant communal sharing.

We found it true, too, that we were only as strong as our neighbors. We would not run away from our neighbors or away from it all. Certainly not away from our homes. We pledged to "stick together" and to "stick it out." Yes, Mississippi was ours too! Many a conversation at Miss Fannie's store focused on this theme.

Our new farm was part of the Old Polk Place, which sometimes was called the Old Polk Plantation. Our new home. There was such beautiful scenery, because we owned it! As we walked to the back fields at sunup each morning, everything around us was simply breathtaking. As a boy, I especially enjoyed walking along the glistening sand at the edges of the creeks. There were and are three different creeks bordering our place. Our place, our creeks—the words had a wonderful sound!

Most mornings the sun glinted on the creek, and the water was the color of sapphires. You could see the water running over two small waterfalls. The water was much fresher in those days too. At other times the clouds blanketed the entire sky except a slit along the horizon through which the sun shined brilliantly, making its final appearance of the day as it sank behind the trees beyond Uncle Nick's house.

During those early morning walks, sunlight created a glimmering path through the water, while reddish purple hues refracted downward so the rippling water in the creeks between the Polks' place and our place and Uncle Nick's place flashed alternate sparkles of bright orange and deep crimson. I never failed to be entranced by these changing colors.

That was a great way to start a morning in the field. But a highlight of the day was looking at and gathering berries in the bountiful wild blackberry patches and the large wild plum patches on Papa's back acres. Here too were those beautiful cotton and corn crops and other crops almost as far as the eye could see. It always delighted us, the way no cityscape ever could.

And right next to the fields in the pasture most days was a lumbering, heavy, yet elegant animal, a bull with a ring through his nose, patiently chewing his cud. The bull belonged to Mr. Holmes. I admired that bull even if, as a young boy, I was a little afraid of him.

And that was, and still is, the physical beauty of our farm and land near Lexington, Mississippi. The vivid wildflowers, the movements of nature, set against the slowness of the country way of living and farm life. This was all anyone could ask for.

Lexington was, and still is, a part of a great America. Holmes County and Mississippi. Just as laid-back today as it was in 1939, when our parents bought our place through the federal Farm Security Administration.

The real beauty of Tchula and Lexington in the old days, to my mind, were the things that money could not buy or build. I remember how wonderful the neighbors were. And the activities of the people themselves. Freeze-framed into my mind and into my memory, too, is the picture of a solitary neighbor plowing against the background of a blazing sunset. And always there are the memories of the picturesque view of Mr. Polk's rolling pastures on the east end of our farm.

But you had to get out into the woods where there were small hidden waterfalls, small caves, and so many unusual flowers and so much greenery to really appreciate the area. During those early years, we kids found remains of graveyards in these woods. Probably slaves, or American Indians, or both.

In addition, we discovered remnants of wine bottles, china—even what we believed to be leftover dinners—buried in a cellar of what we thought were slave quarters. We also found on those grounds drinking gourds and crude wooden bowls. There were bones from all kinds of animals.

At first, in the early 1940s, the clearing around our house was small, and the area thickly wooded. I remember so well a great horned owl which took up residence near our house. You never saw him, but he was living among the pines down near the front creek. His voice from his resting place boomed out, echoing between the hills. He hooted at all sorts of hours, both day and night. As he hooted, we often did our best to imitate and hoot back. And sure enough he replied. He always had the last word.

Sound like a great place? It was. Of course there were some things that today we call inconveniences. Like freezing yourself half to death in the outhouse during the winter. Like no public power or running water. But we had the "running creeks" and springs and a pond. The nearest "good" road was over a bumpy mile and a half away. And another mile and a half to Lexington proper, and on to school.

Of course, heat came from a wood stove and fireplaces. And we had to cut and haul the wood ourselves. We did have a bathroom and tub, but not yet a water heater or plumbing system. Often in the winter, it was necessary to bring water to the house from the creeks and springs.

Our farm was and is physically a glorious place. All of this gave us a feeling of happiness. Of love for the farm. A closeness of family. And, a great appreciation of ownership and pride. We were not sharecroppers or renters any longer. We were landowners!

The community of Balance Due, on the outskirts of Lexington town, near where Papa bought the farm in 1939, now is no more than a few small gardens, a car repair shop among a few permanent homes, and a country store. Poverty and hard times for black people safeguarded this area from the modern world. It did not flourish and grow.

On Miles Hill behind Sweet Holmes Church, the cemetery was filling up. Every week or so, family members or volunteers dug a grave. This was during the 1940s. Fewer black people were being born than died during those times. We were continually reminded of the saying, "Soon there will be no more black people left." Many of the older people often mused that the black "Ten Cup" settlement and another black settlement nicknamed the "School House Bottom" would soon be little more than a row of empty cabins, graveyards, and wagon-wheel ruts in the mud.

Perhaps all of this was said only in nervous jest. For there was always hope. You could see despair but also hope in the eyes of our black neighbors. You could feel it too.

Once there were three times as many people in the community of Balance Due (its real name). At age sixty or so, "Sister Pot Lue" was among the youngest adults left in the community. This stooped woman with fierce, squinty eyes spent her evenings tending her chicken coop, finding time for a little gossiping with her neighbors, across the rails of a rotten wooden fence. She spent most of the day cooking and cleaning house for a white family in town.

For years, the young black people were leaving towns and villages in waves. They left in search of the industrial paradise in places like Memphis and Chicago. And Detroit. During those times, we all talked often about opportunities elsewhere.

In the 1940s neighbors would talk across the fences in black neighborhoods such as Balance Due about President Franklin Delano Roosevelt and how someday he would make it possible for blacks to vote freely. And how black people would surely turn toward the Democratic ticket up North. And away from Lincoln's Republican ticket. Neighbors also talked about possible jobs for young black folks with the CCC and WPA and about FDR's Black Cabinet and Joe Louis, a bright symbol of the times.

But despite this hopeful talk, people were being stripped of many traditions and often their will when they moved to "town" or "upnorth" from the country and from plantations. And "the last to be hired were the first to be fired."

The choices did not really seem to be choices.

In the outlying country areas, the past times of vast inequality haunted a poor everyday life and mocked the dreams of a productive future. An inheritance of dying rural communities matched the urban gloom. In Lexington alone, in addition to Balance Due, there were at least ten other black community scenes of abandonment and poverty.

I still remember old Mrs. Lula Washington sitting on her front proch in Balance Due, yelling at the top of her voice: "Maybe what some people are saying is true, that nothing will ever change, but it is time for us all to start living a real life! We must have faith. We must believe strongly in the future!" Her faith was not enough to save her community. Her exhortations were addressed to the shadows, to the silent shapes of the Mississippi landscapes.

Holmes County, hard-pressed for municipal funds, was forced to slice public school budgets in the 1940s. This was especially tough for black schools, which were already in such bad shape. Many teachers lost their jobs and some schools were closed.

It was a time when everybody had to be strong. And black people were strong. Black people in Mississippi continued to be survivors. It was a time, too, for adults to work harder toward the dream of a better life. To affirm a strong outlook on life for the younger generation. And to establish values that would help black people succeed. "There was no place for hopelessness," my mother, Miss Eva, always said.

In all of the families in our community, there was a strong sense of black history. And every day was a black history day for us kids. There were lessons about the past from our teachers and parents, the kind of push needed to start little black girls and little black boys on to their destinies.

It never occurred to many of us that we would not go on to college after high school in Lexington. For some reason college meant Tuskegee Institute for most of us. It never occurred to many of us, either, that we would not or could not fulfill our goals.

I don't think we actually discussed the merits of attending or not attending college in so many words. It was just what Polks and Archers and Holmeses and Averharts, and all of the others around us, would do. This positive assumption, coupled with a strong sense of historical mission, was what probably made such a difference in our lives.

And our parents and our extended family and those in the community around us and at school and church collectively supplied any additional push we needed. No question but that we believed we would contribute to society and achieve individual success. Many did! Thus, we were urged on to success by family, school, and church, an indomitable triad. Sometimes an especially potent combination, as when Papa himself had an occasion to take to the pulpit. One Sunday Papa was Men Day's speaker at Mount Zion Baptist Church in Tchula. I was so very proud to be in the congregation that Sunday in the early 1940s.

Mount Zion Baptist Church during that time was small but impressive to me: a recently whitewashed, one-room building. Mount Zion was and is located in a colorful area near the base of Sheno Hill where we had previously rented land at the Place. The church attendance on this occasion appeared to have been made up mostly of families sitting together.

The small church had wood shingles painted red, and, as small as it was, had a large parking area for horses, wagons, and cars. Because it was Sunday and because of the oppressive heat, early arrivals for the service moved about slowly and quietly, devoting much of their energy to conversations about family members and other small talk. There was a well for water and a spring of cooler water a few yards into the woods at the west side of the church. Some of the worshipers stopped first at the spring before entering the church. Clustered closely at the base of the same Sheno Hill, just farther along the ridge, were shanty homes of some very poor black families. This to me was a bleak reminder that the church's quaint charm contrasted sharply with a community that had a very definite downside. But I felt myself to be a part of that church, and I remember that special service. Once again I hear my father's voice.

The following is a portion of Papa's speech for that Sunday; his notes have been kept in the family all of these years. This is what he had to say that day:

> It is always so good to be "home" in Tchula. I have gone about churches throughout the county speaking on fellowship and civil rights issues and got many kind welcomes and friendly receptions. But, none touch me as deeply and is heartwarming as greetings from my friends and neighbors here in Tchula. There is no place like "home"! As you probably know, we now live in Lexington. But we are still in Holmes County.
>
> I want to talk today about how "Men and Women Together in Christianity Can Make a Difference." I believe we all can agree that this means everybody. Men. Women. Children. Older folks. The very young. Together in a purpose. Together in God's work. Together in efforts to make this a better place for all.
>
> When I poke into a fire, only the tip of the poker need touch the glowing coal. But, every bit of the poker is involved, and so is the strength of my arm. It seems then that we need to follow the training that Jesus gave the disciples. He pulled them together as strong as a poker. A poker, we might say, made of different metals. Made them into something, by his grace and love, stronger than any one metal before. That united fellowship went out into the world to preach and heal. . . .

I remember well when my oldest son came home from his first day in the first grade at Rose Hill School. I asked him how things went. "Terrible," he said. Naturally, I tried to get to the bottom of his problem, and finally the truth came out. Looking at me, he blurted, "There's three boys and ten million girls!" That was then, of course, and today I'm certain my son would relish those odds. Naturally, he exaggerated, but at that stage of his life, he literally felt overwhelmed by numbers.

Incidentally, that is an easy state to get into. Just get struck in any rush hour leaving Greenwood in a wagon on Saturday evening, and you can easily feel overwhelmeed by numbers.

When we begin feeling that way, it's fairly easy to begin thinking that we as black people are insignificant. We each think, I have only one wagon among all these other cars and wagons leaving. What can I do? I'm only one driver among all of these others on the street. What can I do? I'm the only black person among all the human beings on this planet. What can I do?

Yes, it's easy to feel that way. When we see ourselves as tiny and unimportant. When we see ourselves as not mattering in the framework of everything. When we begin to look at what we do as little and unimportant, especially in a racist and unfeeling world of white people; when we do these things, it is easy to adopt an attitude of "Why bother? It doesn't matter anyhow."

It does not have to be that way. The answer to all of this is, "Think men and women together in Christ." Together, we can make a big difference. Even then, we could all feel that we are insignificant from time to time—we wouldn't be human if we didn't. It is important, however, that we recognize this feeling for what it is—a momentary setback; a time when the pressure of unequal and unfair treatment to a people for so long has gotten to us.

It is a time when we are momentarily overwhelmed by the demands of a day-by-day, prejudiced world. At times like these, we must remember that everything we do as a group, and what we do, makes a difference for our people everywhere. For all people. It makes a difference now, and tomorrow, and the day after.

Yes, together we can make a difference—each and every one of us. In an effort to make a better world. For all. If we give up, if we feel that we cannot make a difference, then the difference we make will be a negative one. If, however, we know that what we do together will have a positive effect tomorrow and tomorrow and tomorrow, we will then do our best at all times, and that best certainly will make a beneficial and glowing contribution to Mount Zion Baptist Church, to the community, to Tchula, to Holmes County, to America, and to the world. . . .

It has been said that to get anywhere in this world as black people, you have to know someone important—we do—we have to know *ourselves*. Knowing ourselves as a whole church, whole town, and whole neighborhood; knowing what we can and cannot do as a church and as a people, and trying to be our best in each and every situation; believing that what we can do today is important and will affect tomorrow; we must strive with this in mind to do what we can.

Again, doing all of this will make this world a better place for anyone in it. This is especially true for us black people. Just imagine a church in Tchula, Mississippi, or a world filled with people who know that what they do will make a difference, and who strive consciously to make that difference a positive good for everyone. This can bring about a world of freedom within our grasp. We, together, do make a difference, and that difference is within us.

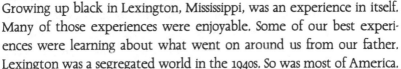

Growing up black in Lexington, Mississippi, was an experience in itself. Many of those experiences were enjoyable. Some of our best experiences were learning about what went on around us from our father. Lexington was a segregated world in the 1940s. So was most of America. But no one could tell our parents what to think. Or say. Or pass on to us. They gave us strength, and a sense of community.

Some Sunday evenings the whole family sat together under the pecan trees on the back lawn and watched the clouds change into whatever our imaginations came up with. Two bales of cotton. A tractor or barn, a mule or a beautiful saddle horse. Symbols of freedom in the Mississippi clouds.

We would sit facing our rolling pasture seeing or imagining the long and promising vistas that lay beyond. Usually during the summer months it was hot. Real hot. The humidity was sometimes so thick we could almost roll it in our hands. Then, the Delta thunderstorms and warm rain often drove us inside.

Papa—"Mr. Chat," as he was so fondly called during his adult years—was both a participant and observer in our children's games and our neighborhood life, and he understood the larger world. Our talks outgrew the cloud games. We often discussed how slavery molded the minds of people through the years. How it molded the thinking of both white and black people. Rich and poor, northern and southern people. We discussed the many whip-cracking plantation overseers of just a few years past. We talked about the ones who were still around. Our father also taught us how to think positive thoughts about black culture and black life, and about faith, hopes, and dreams and inspirations for coming generations.

As a family, we wondered together about the wave of black people moving to the North during the Second World War and the disappointment and frustration caused by racial discrimination in those other places far from our place.

Many an evening at Miss Fannie Golden's store, the regular "grown-up group" talked about these and other things. The group was Uncle Perry and Uncle Nick, and Mr. Polk and Mr. Averhart, and other regulars. And Papa. They talked about how hundreds of thousands of blacks were serving in the segregated armed forces—with distinction. Mr. Averhart was one of the first of any race in all of Mississippi to have a Blue Star in his window. To lose a son in the fight for democracy.

They talked about positive things, too, such as the then increasing literacy. But more often about limited economic opportunities and about Jim Crow. And we kids would listen.

Miss Fannie's was a small, rural, relaxed, black "mom and pop" store with a warm and happy atmosphere. Miss Fannie sold bologna sandwiches and RC colas, cinnamon rolls, and roasted peanuts. And pickled pig feet, a favorite item among her regular groceries.

Papa always brought each of us a treat from the store on Saturday nights. He never once missed. Miss Fannie's store offered cold colas and a forum for the discussion of hopes and dreams. And treats for us kids.

There was always hope in our hearts in Lexington during the 1940s. It was a time of faith in the future and hope for a fair way of life, someday, in America. Lexington communities were tinged with sadness; some, like Balance Due, were dying places, but some were sufficiently buttressed by dreams to endure.

10 On Education (and Mama)

 The early schools that I attended were the same type of one-room church school that my father attended at Mount Olive. (See the photograph of the interior of a typical school in Holmes County.) But unlike students at Mount Olive school, I had Mama and a cousin, Ethel Speed, as teachers at my first school, Rose Hill. But the school had the same type of potbellied wood stove that Papa's school had and it often became the students' lot to find wood to make fires and maintain them to heat the school in cold weather.

After moving to Lexington from the Place near Tchula, I attended Ambrose Vocational High School. This was the same school that Mama had attended and its physical condition had not been improved much from the time of the earlier generation. When Mama attended this school it was called Lexington Graded School and only went through the eleventh grade.

The school was later named for its fourth principal, Daniel W. Ambrose, and the twelfth grade was added to its curriculum. Ambrose was overcrowded almost from the beginning of its existence. Nevertheless, Ambrose did a surprisingly good job of student training, even though it was not meant to be an academic school. Blacks in Mississippi—both in my youth and when my parents were students—were not thought to need an academic high school, because they were not supposed to be intellectually capable of absorbing anything but vocational training.

Although an extra grade was added to the school's curriculum, its general condition remained the same until the state legislature decided that it would improve the educational facilities for black people. That happened only in the 1950s, after the Supreme Court overturned the separate but equal doctrine under which the South's citizens had lived. After this decision, Mississippi decided to build better schools for black people throughout the state.

It is painfully evident that generations of black people are suffering today because Mississippi did not provide adequate schools for its black citizens. Granted, the quality of public education for all of America's students has come under fire. But Mississippi's black citizens have fared worse than those of almost any other state. The state has yet to move from the bottom rung of states in terms of educational facilities.

During my time at Ambrose I had to walk over three and one-half miles to and from school. I had to walk an extra three-quarters of a mile solely because I was black. Lexington High School, the white school, was that much closer than Ambrose, but I, of course, could not attend Lexington High. Even when the county started running school buses, they were only for whites. These buses passed right in front of my home to pick up two white students who lived about one-half mile beyond my home, but black students were not even allowed to ride in the back of these buses. One superintendent of education made a point of announcing to us that "you blacks will never ride in those yellow buses." (After I graduated, buses were later provided for black students in certain areas of the county.)

Having said this, I want to emphasize that many of us did manage to get more than an adequate education. In fact, some of us received a very good education, thanks to some exceptional and highly dedicated teachers.

Mama had a special dedication to education and the rewards that an education could bring. She started teaching before she graduated from high school, an accepted though not too common practice.

After attending a small college in Mississippi for two years Mama started teaching in earnest at various church schools including Mount

Olive Church School, which Papa had attended. During the summer vacations, between the times all of us children were born, Mama earned her bachelor's degree at Alcorn State University in Mississippi, Indiana University, Mississippi State University, and Catholic University of America.

Mama worked ten years or more at various county schools, including a short tenure at her alma mater and mine, Ambrose; after that, she joined the staff of Saints Industrial and Literary School, a private church-run school in Lexington. This school was a boarding and day school that included grades one through twelve. Mama taught math and held numerous other positions.

Saints, as the school was always called, was the first black high school to achieve full academic accreditation in our area and one of the first in the state of Mississippi. Saints was the first school in the area to have a completely equipped library and science facilities. Many family memories are there.

Recently my mother and I were sitting at the kitchen table, at home in Lexington. If we are not eating at the table we're just talking, and vice versa. Eat and talk, that is mostly what we do. Mama will ask me questions like: "How was your year—good, bad, or indifferent? Did you accomplish what you wanted to? Were there some unexpected stumbling blocks? How did you handle them? What would you do differently?" Most of all, she will say, "Did you at least have some fun during the year? Are you able to look back and see the humor in even the serious situations?"

The dishes had been cleared from breakfast, and in their place on the table we brought out memories. On this occasion we thought and talked about school, and teachers. Favorite teachers we had admired close to fifty years before, and still admire today.

Teachers like Almeta Coleman Polk, our neighbor and fourth-grade teacher at Ambrose Vocational Elementary School. Of course the school was all black when she taught there in the 1940s. Her school was a wooden building not too different from those of thousands of other schools in a thousand other places even today. The elementary school, separate from the high school, was a six-teacher building with a vocational section, small lunchroom, and very small auditorium. There was no library.

Mrs. Polk could be seen and heard leading her fourth-grade class through the previous night's homework. The students joyfully participated. Mama recalled one time when two little girls giggled inattentively, and a student assistant who was a senior from the high school whispered from the back of the room, "Now you girls pay attention!" It was a loud stage whisper, but, as told, they turned around and listened.

Even to the casual observer, one could see that the class was alive with learning. Mrs. Polk was an unmistakably competent and caring teacher. A teacher who looked to the future and taught her students vision too. She saw the world as a positive and exciting arena for learning. Her pupils in the fourth grade were lucky to have her.

Mrs. Polk was known to discuss "life things" like values, goals, and the future. She often voiced the hope that her students someday would have a freer and better life. They were told, at that early age, that someday they themselves "would have the power to make changes for the greater good." Along with decimals, long division, and handwriting, she tried to communicate a future that was wonderful and full of choices. "We all must get away from volunteer slavery," she often said.

"My students will not be taught with the assumption that they will grow up to serve. They are taught the fact that they can be what they want to be. To be leaders. Their foundations will be such that they can go on to any program, school, or career that they so desire. We are building citizens here!" she would say emphatically.

"We must teach the whole person, physically and mentally," she would continue. And she meant what she said. Mrs. Polk led frequent field trips. Her class went on excursions all over the county. She and her pupils built their own small greenhouse and filled it with lots of plants. She used an old building to demonstrate life in a slave cabin. Her teaching method personified the "living history" approach. If the textbook talked about candlemaking, the class made candles. She was not locked into a rigid curriculum.

School programs for black children all over the South often trained them to work only in the rural and small-town environment in which we lived. That is, farming and service-related jobs only. The name of our school itself, Ambrose Vocational, meant the school's primary objective was related to the trades. Not academic or what one might think of as preparation for higher academic training.

Mrs. Polk worked to do something about all of this. Her candlemaking project, and the greenhouse, and the fourth-grade "slave cabin" were all part of something bigger. As Mama has often pointed out to me, those activities were part of Mrs. Polk's plan to help kids think, write, speak, and live.

In high school, we had teachers like Jim Davis, who gave us attention both as individuals and as a group. He did his very best, under the circumstances, to help us develop an ability to reason objectively and methodically. And to provide us with an acceptable preparation for college.

Teachers did all they could to prevent a self-induced expectation of failure on our part. They required more and more from us. And impressed upon us that at no time should we take a backseat to any other group of students, or anyone else, for that matter. And to never, never, buy into the notion that we were intellectually inferior—the fact that we were faced with separate but unequal schools notwithstanding.

Our teachers did things like making us aware of long-term career goals, as opposed to short-term goals. Mrs. N. Thomas Davis, the wife of Mr. Davis, made a point of stressing to the girls that they must realize the fact that poor, never married black mothers were less likely to move on to a better life than married ones.

Mrs. Davis let female students know, too, that unmarried mothers' children were most likely to be whittled down by economic deprivation. And that for many such young women, the best they could look forward to was the worst society had to offer. That the loss of the black family, in any form, was a stark tragedy.

"Black women were not put on this earth just to have babies—especially while near babies yourselves. Even if the slave owners may have thought so," counseled Mrs. Davis. I had the pleasure of listening in on some of her pep talks to the girls.

Every teacher often reminded us, too, that poor English was a legacy of a slavery system that made education an unlawful benefit for black people to have. And that we must not let poor English be passed on by generations of the unschooled and improperly educated who spoke it.

Daily, teachers at Ambrose Vocational High School dealt with helping us learn things about life and about ourselves. Things that we didn't know, but could learn most often from them. They always seemed to be able to find new ways to help us build self-confidence and to really stretch our potential, helping us do our part in making America a better nation. And, if you ever had any problems at all, you knew that you could go to them.

Dorothy Hamilton Talbert, our home economics and health education teacher, was a woman with extraordinary talent, especially skilled at teaching girls quilt making as an art form. She was also an articulate spokesperson for quilt making as an art, one that was *and still is* deeply rooted in black culture.

Mrs. Talbert got students interested in creating quilts with narratives. Some depicted events, such as important moments of the life of Booker T. Washington—as a tribute to Dr. Washington and other black figures of the times. She taught the art of quilt making, and the art of storytelling, in an accessible, visual form.

In Mrs. Talbert's classes we learned how to read the labels on canned food and to shop for nutritional food. With the help of this innovative teacher, we constructed a "healthy food choices" kit—made up of daily activities that could be used in our class on nutrition, such as visiting our own gardens, keeping a food diary, and learning table manners. We practiced lots of dining etiquette. A good idea fifty years ago, and not a bad idea in the 1990s!

***

Mama and I both recall the first day of school in the fall of 1942.

Cash from ginned cotton seeds was paid the same day to farmers who owned their land and sold their own crops. Father needed the seed money for our school clothes and supplies. That first bale of cotton would bring that necessary money for school. Credit was next to impossible for black people. "Unless you sold your birthright," Papa always said. However, that year, rain delayed the harvest. The first bale of cotton was completed about one week later. So we had to wait a week longer for school supplies.

I remember that first day of school, waiting in the kitchen for the rest of the Archer kids to get ready. In about one hour, yellow public school buses would rumble up the road to pick up white children. They would not slow down one bit for children already starting their three-and-a-half-mile walk to Holmes County's one black public school. White people had several schools. School buses were for white children alone. It was as simple as that.

Farmers were under lots of pressure to keep children old enough to work the fields—in the fields. Many of us remember how those pressures translated into tenant farmer evictions, food credit cutoffs, and peoples' relatives losing jobs in retaliation against those who simply sent their children to school.

All around, preparation of black children in the three Rs had to yield to demands of a sharecropper economy. But parents and teachers knew well that knowledge and education were essential for the future of black people. They never ceased pulling against all odds. So we walked to school, and waited until the cotton crop came in to pay for new pencils. But go to school we did. That was never an issue.

When we opened falling-apart, hand-me-down history books from white public schoolchildren later that morning, we found no information about black people. There was nothing about black artists, writers, scientists, political leaders, or military heroes. Unless we learned about them at home or directly from our teachers, we had no role models to admire and emulate. At the time, however, on the first day of school, I mainly worried about the rain. And the cotton. School supplies and heroes would come later.

Many remember so well, too, a March school day in 1943, perhaps for some of us as if it was yesterday, when teacher, students, and parents alike talked about Marian Anderson, whose voice Arturo Toscanini described as appearing once in a century. Discussions of the incident took almost two whole class periods.

Miss Anderson was refused permission to sing in Constitution Hall in Washington by the Daughters of the American Revolution. Many of us also remember well how the whole student body of Ambrose High and the entire neighborhood celebrated after a later Anderson concert held at the Lincoln Memorial drew seventy-five thousand people on Easter.

Our teachers took the time to remind us that we should search for anything in the form of historical symbols that would reinforce our cultural realities. That it was all right to be proud of Abraham Lincoln and George Washington, but that as black people, we needed much more. We needed to identify with persons like Miss Anderson.

Our teachers told us, too, that it was important to appreciate our talents and the talents of those around us. We learned about our own bluesman B. B. King, who was about that time cutting his first record. I think our class was one of the first to hear the recording, which may have been titled "Delta Boy Blues." What I am sure of is that the record was full of unadorned country blues sounds, some familiar, some obscure to us as students, but all performed without the slightest hint of wile. In those days, the first thing that you noticed about B. B. was his voice—"down-home," husky, and haunting, and it was not one you were likely to question. No matter how sad or outrageous the tale he was telling in song.

Our teachers taught us to learn from artists like B. B. King. B. B. was a real live role model. There was that acoustic guitar playing we could strive for. There were the staccato accents, loping bass lines, jabbing side riffs, and the neat turnarounds that set up each of B. B.'s verses. As a teenager, I was dazzled by his sounds.

Like B. B., his songs were deeply rooted in Mississippi and in the rural South and evoked a distinct sound of the era. I am happy that our teachers at Ambrose Vocational High School encouraged us to appreciate black art forms, including jazz and country blues.

How little the world really knows of the way things were in the 1940s in Lexington. How devoid of everyday detail is the world's knowledge of events there a little less than fifty years ago. But it is nice to remember that at Ambrose Vocational High School we had the pleasure of discovering Marian Anderson and B. B. King.

One day at the breakfast table Mama gave me a sly smile and asked, "Remember the graduation play?"

Oh, yes, indeed I do. I can never forget "The Archers' Ghost," which inspired the play that was the capstone of my senior year.

In May 1946, at Ambrose Vocational High School, the feeling of graduation was in the air for seniors. Sorphonia Moses, our homeroom teacher and English teacher, had a megaphone resting across her lap as she sat wearily that late afternoon in the wooden seats in the front row of the auditorium. I can see her now, watching us. For the last time, we had rehearsed our play, "Haunted Slave Hut on Elm Road," written by the senior class.

The play was based on a local legend that came to be known as The Archers' Ghost. The play was about a haunted hut on the farm we rented years before near Tchula. It was all about a log cabin that was 150 years old. There were strange goings-on in and around the hut that stood in a pasture with acres of farmland in all directions. There were restless spirits, bedeviled children, and frightened adults.

Mrs. Moses, who served as sponsor of the play, was exhausted from weeks of long, trying practices and rehearsals. Her colleague Dewitt Townsend, on the other hand, moved across the room at a frenzied pace, moving the few lights we had, fixing props, keeping order, and talking to us somewhat irritated, tired, and hungry students. Mr. Townsend and the rest of the teachers in the school were willing to do whatever they could to make the play a success. The teachers also wanted us to display our special talents and abilities. They took special pride in us. The players, most of us seniors, poured ourselves into the characters we would become and the lines we would recite on the following evening. We became more than players on a stage.

I believe I was the first to tell the tale of The Archers' Ghost to fellow students some years before. The story grew after that. It became part of our oral archives. The story—and the play—went more or less like this:

The log hut on our rented farm had no windows. But it did have strong shutters with wooden latches. The hut was one with a wooden floor and brick chimney. It also had a kitchen and two bedrooms, a double outhouse, and a cistern. All of these were quite unusual as slave huts went. And 150 years later the cabin was as sturdy and strong as ever. Eerie. It appeared that someone or something was keeping the deserted place in good repair.

The story went that a white slave master many years before killed his son by his black mistress because the child was deformed. The mother was also said to have grieved herself to death shortly afterward. The story goes on to say that the master disappeared without a trace. According to legend, he was never seen again.

There is one small mound and a larger one on the north side of the slave hut that we young Archers believed to be graves. Tip, our dog, and Uncle Nick's dog, Collie, would go anyplace about the premises except near those mounds. Nor would any other dog, so far as we knew, get close to the mounds. They'd just stand at a distance and bark. On the other hand, residents on the Place reported at different times that they had seen untraceable dog prints near the "graves." There were never any prints leading to or going away from the sites.

The ghosts of the mother and her baby long haunted the slave hut on Elm Road. Everybody who saw her reported that she was always dressed in misty white and always cradled what was presumed to be her baby, bundled in her arms. She would be seen walking lightly but steadily along Elm Road close to a stream, looking neither to the right nor left. Many reported that she had fierce, haunting brown eyes with illuminating, mysterious luster. They really glowed. We two eldest kids in the family would attest to this. We both saw her at the same time.

The road curved near a small bridge and there the beautiful woman disappeared for a second, to reappear at the cistern in back of the hut, still clasping the ghostly child in her arms. Finally the pair would walk a short distance toward some woods near the hut and disappear. The story was that the pair was trying to get to Rose Hill Church.

Uncle Perry, our leader on the Place, let a homeless couple, Sally and Edwin Walker, and their three children stay in the hut once free of rent. They stayed less than two months. No other persons we knew of ever lived there. This family told some pretty weird stories.

The Walker family kept a kerosene lamp on the mantel at night. Often the lamp would go flying across the room and crash. The family said it would "just fly." They never saw anything, but they heard footsteps going in and out of the back door of the cabin. They also heard snoring, talking, and hard breathing.

Mrs. Walker told us that once when alone in the hut, "I decided to light and bank a fire. The night before had been chilly. That is when a series of knocks began. It was just past dawn. I realized that the knocking was coming from the right-hand side of the fireplace, just above my head."

As brave and levelheaded as Sally Walker thought she was, she admitted that "the blood in my veins began to run cold, my skin tightened across my skull, I felt ice forming in my cheeks. My hands began to tremble." The knocking ceased, but her physical symptoms did not. "For a moment or so I thought that I was rooted to the spot," she said. "I wanted to run, but my legs would not do what I told them." She never went near the hut or the site after that. The whole family moved in with others in Tchula the following week.

My aunt Mama Jane, who was regarded as a psychic, maintained that the hut and surrounding area were taken over by spirits. The beautiful dead woman, according to Mama Jane, was "female energy."

"The spirits," she would insist, "will not accept their deaths, but are friendly and would not harm anyone. But they could cause people to hurt themselves."

After we moved to Lexington, there were reports that strange noises were still heard at the site, and that the lovely woman and her baby were sighted again. They are still said to be occasionally seen today. It seems that restless spirits are still in or around that slave hut.

The play was a huge success. After the performance, boys and girls who were graduating seniors got together in Tchula for a "down-home" country breakdown. The party was at the home of Mr. Joe, the "Blues Man," and was to celebrate graduation day and the play.

We knew that this group of musicians and their friends would create a lively spirit of houseparty blues. They were masters of the down-home blues tradition. The party was a success too. That was my first houseparty, but by no means the last. That first party grew into a lifetime of blues houseparties for me.

I realized, later, that those gatherings communicated our values and history, our good and bad times, and gave us a real sense of community.

And our Archer ghost story and the play were part of a growing legacy of black folks' stories, music, and dance to be shared in the years to come.

Our "special learning places" out on our farm were the pond and creeks and the cotton rows.

We learned how many things fit together. In nature and in other realms. And how to relate one experience to another as a process in building a good learning foundation. And how to profit from those experiences. Our father believed that this was true education, whether in school or outdoors on the farm.

We simply learned from everything. Even from frogs and toads. Mother had us set up a home for about a dozen large frogs and toads, making a pool for them, with big pieces of wood and rocks for frog sunbathing. We made other pools for tadpoles at various stages of growth. We were then able to talk more observantly about their activities, how life within the ponds went on, and how changes came about.

Mama, a schoolteacher as always, pointed out the differences between toads and frogs and drew our attention to peculiarities of their habits. We wrote down what we saw and learned. It was much fun. Inspired by frogs, we also read books about them. The best part, though, was building their pools.

We took time to talk about what we learned during the week each Sunday afternoon. The only requirement for Sunday's presentations was that we talk about five things we learned at home during the week. Not new facts from school, but discoveries made right at home. It's a simple teaching technique I would recommend to every family.

Proud times were when no one missed a single day from school during the school year. And when we earned good grades. But the most important thing was that we all did the very best that we could. All of us did not make top grades at school, not by any means. But we learned to wonder about everything. During those times it was necessary for families to strongly support schools and supplement their teachings. Papa did this through his conversations with us, whenever one or more of us would follow him up and down the cotton rows while he was plowing. When he would stop to rest the mules, it would be time for a chat. And Mama did it through her frogs, and through her question-and-answer sessions at the kitchen table, a tradition that continues to this day.

11 Black/White

Life in Lexington at times was such a contrast. Such a contrast from when we lived at the Place in Tchula. We were now here in this town without the protection of rural isolation, without the protective coloration of fields and woods or the comforting ambience of our totally black hamlet. I was now old enough to feel the "hate stare" of white people. I felt for the first time the always pervading animosity and differentness. Our moving to a larger town brought new definitions and new dimensions of racism: the squalor of places like Black Tin Cup Alley and the regular violence on Saturday nights. And yet these Lexington years were also a time when courage and dreams outweighed fears. A time of strong faith. Of positive ambitions, determination, and directions for a black population of young people, and their elders too.

These years were the season for taking advantage of any opportunities, say, the chance to go to high school and even on to college. And for making the best of bad situations. As young as I was, I realized that it was necessary to make our own future regardless of odds. And that we had to keep up the belief that someday blacks would become a partner in the American dream.

We black children in Lexington were not allowed in the town's public library, the public park, or the zoo. Nor through the front door of any white person's house. It was an era when we were required to leave the sidewalk when meeting white people. We children learned there were colored and white drinking fountains in front of the courthouse on the square. We learned of "separate but equal" facilities throughout Mississippi.

It was a time when solid segregation and lynchings infested the South. A time of continued vicious racism and economic oppression for black people, of poll taxes and Jim Crow laws. A dollar bill taken by a white person directly from the hand of a black person in Lexington or Tchula stores was treated as if it had a disease. But never, never refused.

Sam James, a neighbor of ours, knocked on our door and awoke our family on an early September morning and told us breathlessly that an all-white jury had acquitted a rural sheriff the day before. The sheriff had been charged with shooting a handcuffed black prisoner four times. Although there were white as well as black witnesses to the crime, the acquittal was almost inevitable. Sam James told us what in our hearts we already knew.

It was an age when children and teenagers in Lexington were often held in the city jail for no reason other than to be "taught lessons." It was a time when police would brutally bend wrists and fingers of black people. Stories from jail were a litany of pain and unusual punishments. I personally still feel the splitting pain inflicted by the police only because I did not get off the sidewalk while passing a white woman.

I remember a "show and tell" in our homeroom at Ambrose Vocational High School. Curtis Winston, my classmate, had this story to tell one morning: two days before, he was slapped and struck by a white kid and called names. Curtis slapped and struck back. The other kid promptly reported the incident to his father. The father waited for, and caught up with, Curtis on his way home from school the next afternoon. The father forced Curtis to come with him upstairs above the black pool room on Beale Street. Curtis's wrists were tied behind him with a block and tackle attached to the rope. Curtis was then hoisted up on tiptoe with his feet almost clear of the floor. The father kept him there while he screamed, "You son of a bitch, I will teach you to hit my son. Just wait until I get my bullwhip. Now you stay right there until I get back." Luckily, the man did not come back within a reasonable time. Some black men arrived on the scene and cut Curtis down. My classmate had badly scarred wrists to show.

White officers used handcuffs so tight that black wrists became swollen, sometimes broken, and then tightened more. Black people were not permitted to see a lawyer when charged with a crime.

Anyway, life had to go on. The physical South in the 1930s was a slow, charming, and pretty place. The mild climate and a certain rural richness gave the Deep South its fabled, languorous beauty. We talked about and appreciated all of this. In the 1930s there was much love for the land. Love for the climate and the bounty of the land. Love for the warm, pleasant charm and slow way of life that made the Delta so beguiling.

But there was also angry talk, about many other things. Oh, the bitter voices and anger because of the region's insufferable treatment of black people. The prejudice and discrimination. And Tchula Lake. That beautiful yet notorious Tchula Lake! The waters where so many black men and women disappeared.

People sometimes stopped at the Tchula Lake bridge to watch for the body of a black person who had been killed in the night and dumped off the bridge to float on the surface of the water by dawn, before being pulled out. Yet, despite the sight of a black body floating in our beloved and sometimes hated lake, there were always talks about "keeping on."

And there was always talk about things that we youngsters were not supposed to hear. Much was supposed to be "adult talk" since it was of violence, insults to black people, and continual humiliations.

As children, we were aware of visitors from Chicago, New York City, and other places, who said things such as "I would like to see the town of Tchula blasted by dynamite until not one building is left standing!" These were the types of feelings that most people voiced on coming back to Mississippi during the 1930s and 1940s.

There was always talk about families who were trying ever so hard to leave the South. Most young people left with no intentions of coming back except for brief visits to their families. Yes, what we heard constantly was that when black people left the South it was forever.

The emigrants said they hated the South for what they had suffered physically and spiritually, and that they were eager to take part in any and all efforts to fight the things for which the South stood.

Mostly, people wanted to get their families out of the South, to "freed" territory where they were no longer "boys," "gals," "uncles," and "aunts." To a place where they were not in an atmosphere of constant repression and occasional terror. They talked of escaping the maddening, smug assumption of white "superiority," and the transparent condescension of "good" white folks who "always loved black people."

Talk also was of everyday, commonplace treatment of people who stayed behind in Mississippi. There was talk of the fact that most whites apparently did not know that blacks who were left behind also loathed Dixie's "institutions" and vestigial, plantation ways of life. Talk was about how grown people were forced to swallow their pride and keep on going, making the best of things. Making the best of the worst. For three centuries, blacks in the Deep South fought their way to freedom. First by religion and hope, then by rebellion and resistance and flight. And in the 1930s and 1940s by education and organization and hard work.

This was a time when Mississippi was the only state where black people were systematically excluded from the polls. Here we were prevented illegally from voting by the arbitrary whim of Holmes County officials, and by threats and violence. The poll tax still existed. Literacy and "understanding" tests prevented black people from voting. Unfortunately, one of our biggest deterrents to the vote at that time appeared to be the lack of people actually attempting to register. Mostly, I believe, they were prevented from registering through subtle coercion.

Strange as it may seem, whites badly wanted black people's acceptance. White people wanted us to assure them that everything was fine with us. "You are alive and happy!" we heard from them often. Yes, we were alive. Safe and secure? No. Content? No. As human beings, we did not lose hope of someday being able to just visit the public library of our choice. Or any library at all, for that matter.

We desperately wanted to just feel safe from abuse when we walked down the street. To be able to look in a shop window, or just watch the sunset, without worry about physical harm. To have entitlements the same as other people. To have the same opportunities as other races whose kids were born with an edge so comprehensive as to constitute unlimited entitlement.

We wondered all the time. We wondered why such a terrible thing as this state of conditions, as a people, had to happen to us? Why did we have to live in a place where black people were forever in fear of the rest of society?

Now, there is one thing our family never did—we never wondered if life was worth living. On the other hand, we knew about and read about noteworthy local whites ending it all. For them, the death of the antebellum culture was too painful to bear. Those suicides had a sobering effect on each of us.

We all were well aware that conditions in the Delta were the result of the lingering impact of years of slavery, racism, and discrimination. Legalized racial segregation took its toll on all of Mississippi's citizens, black and white alike.

Yet, with all of this, there is today true and deep affection for places where we once lived. Our family had been around Holmes County since slavery days.

Most of us in a younger generation were baptized not very far from where our grandfathers and grandmothers were baptized in a creek near Funny Gusher Hill. Near Rose Hill Church. We kids fished with poles and sanded for fish with nets at that creek while growing up. And once I visited the spot during a break from school. Holmes County was a place where we toiled, spent a lot of time just working and surviving, where we helped our families to eke out a living. So there were many contradictions. Regardless of circumstances, there was that basic attachment to the land, to Mississippi.

Love of land! There was a certain enjoyment of it all around us while we were growing up. In the form of nature—in the form of spring planting and its fury, and the tensions of ministering unto crops and truckpatches. I look back fondly today on how the small amount of machinery we owned kept breaking down, how the ground was either too wet or too dry. How we had not been able to buy needed seeds on time, how other seeds were crying to be planted. How what we tried to do was always too hopeful, and each day the sun set too soon.

We balanced hope for another good year against a crop washout. There was a pure joy in just watching the truck garden's young seedlings open. Open with their elegant and unique blooms.

Many questions we raised could not easily be resolved, for the questions involved everything wrong in America at that time. The questions touched on everything social, economic, political. And America certainly had a lot of problems in all those areas.

Even though I am painfully aware of, and remember well, the hardships and mistreatment that all black people went through in Tchula, I still return to Mississippi often. I visited some "special" spots there recently. One special spot was where I raised a special kind of eggplant called Black Beauty. I remember so well that the vegetable had a great taste; it was hearty, handsome to look at, and not difficult to grow. Something about the place, or lots of things, keep calling me back.

School was out for the day. I was walking home, sometimes jogging, but mostly just thinking, whistling, and looking. The experiences this particular day were a somewhat odd mixture. A young black lad's adventures.

At the time, I thought how nice it would be to live next door to Ambrose Vocational High School, the black public school I was just leaving. If I lived close to school, I would not have to walk the more than three and a half miles each morning and afternoon.

The three school buildings at Ambrose housed all grades from first through twelfth. That day Miss Presley's citizenship class was about preparation for voting and citizenship. I was in sixth or seventh grade at the time. For some of the memories, I say thank you. For some I don't.

There was indeed young hope voiced by all of us who participated in our class discussions on that day. The hope that black people would soon be voting freely. Miss Presley talked a lot about the voting process, and we all discussed people's capacity to make sound decisions when they voted.

Important points were made by both the class and teacher regarding the fact that citizens should be knowledgeable about basic facts of government. Our teacher told us, "So as not to be limited in our ability to interpret events and to understand how American government works, we must be well prepared." We also discussed the way presidential candidates were nominated by national party conventions. And during the day's discussions, the teacher put lots of emphasis on factors that made human freedom possible.

The settlement that surrounded Ambrose High was totally black. It was affectionately known as the School House Bottom. The black people's neat shotgun houses with well-swept yards were close to Ambrose High. Beyond these houses were many ramshackle, low-ceilinged wooden huts built at the turn of the century or earlier— homes for many.

Then came the white folks' homes, some of which might be called mansions. Theirs were the brick or large frame houses. Most of their houses were of red brick and located a few blocks from the town square.

The road leading home began at the turnoff to Castillian Road, just before the Church of God and Christ, and one mile south of the town square on Highway 17. It was supposed to be graveled, but was mostly dirt and badly washed out.

It was the type of rough road that was at the point of threatening injury to people riding in wagons, buggies, or ox carts. I thought it remarkable at the time that alongside those rough roads ran telephone lines from tree to tree, from post to post. We young people enjoyed the constant humming of the wires.

Beginning at the turnoff, the way was rough. The road was not much better than those in the unimproved countryside, especially in the springtime. As I happily moved on down the road toward home, I took a shortcut through two oak trees, not too far from the golf course (white only), skirting the streams and small creeks with their heavy thickets. Until a few years earlier, this area was impenetrable.

Even at that time long stretches seemed almost untouched. On the surrounding land, a few cows grazed.

I thought to myself at the time, this area was a wild and wonderful playground. It was lots of fun for me to establish a closeness to such wonderful new surroundings. Never was I so happy! Nature all around me, and so much to learn. Especially from nature.

That day, still looking at the beautiful scenery very close to our house, and daydreaming as usual, I continued along. I suddenly looked up and saw an old black man so fair, of such ghostly pallor, that one could hardly tell that he was not white.

The old man stood in the nearby creek bed, his trousers rolled to his ankles, his legs spread for balance. He stood in the creek, startled and frozen as a deer in midleap, the water rippling over his feet. He did not seem exactly "real." Not a word did he speak, although I spoke to him. That was the one time I really wished that I owned a Brownie camera like my older cousin Tommie. I would have recorded the encounter for posterity.

The old man was something to see. Then he moved on; he did not break his even stride or even glance my way. I called out to him, but he said nothing. He continued up on the sandy creek bed. Broad of back, with straight gray-black hair, he stood straight as a rod while he looked only toward the path in between the small hills leading to our house.

Many years have passed since then, but I can't forget the old man. I remember that scene best of all. It was the most vivid of the day. I never saw the old man before, and I never saw him again. And yet, I somehow still feel a strange kinship with him. Perhaps because he fit the exact description of my uncle Josh, long dead at the time, on my mother's side of the family. Seeing the old man made the woods magical.

Still on the way home, I stopped a moment to talk with my father. I saw him plowing, just beyond the woods. A flock of hens followed along, almost under the hooves of Papa's mules, old King and Queen, as he plowed that day. The mules stirred up tidbits in the soil eagerly noted by the hens.

The fields and woods were an open book and Papa, as usual, was my teacher. He would point out huge, luscious wild plums and strawberries in the low fields and near the creeks. A thicket of blackberry brambles "shut off from the rest of the world" was only about fifty steps from where Papa was plowing.

Right under our feet was the "richest soil in the world," Papa always said. "The right soil makes all the difference. The larger corn, hay, and cotton crops are just the same as planting a garden." He would emphasize, "To enjoy an abundant harvest, you've got to start with fertile soil."

I doubt I could even find that exact patch of woods and field today. Still, when the spring and autumn begin to lure me home to Lexington today, I still see the birds and the wild plums in my mind's eye and can hear the sounds of the creek. I see Papa sitting on the plow for a second of rest, or walking steadily behind old Queen and King. And I remember how that afternoon I rushed to catch up with my father, to tell him about the old man in the creek, my black/white ghost.

Springtime in Lexington was a season of kaleidoscopic growth. Cedars and oaks provided a lush green cover all over the area. The pathways along the creeks and small rivers were bursting with red, yellow, and blue wildflowers. Everything that survived the brutal December frost was alive and flourishing. That year, 1940, black people hoped so much for a bright light at the end of a dark tunnel. The 1940s seemed to be a promising new decade.

However, in 1940, we black people in Lexington, Mississippi, were not in a condition that could even remotely be called free. Severe racial restrictions were still in place. To keep us "in our place," black people had to always address white people as "Mister," "Madam," "Miss," and so on. Black people also had to take off their hats in greeting whites. We boys had to learn this at an early age. Black people were not to expect whites to ever shake their hands and were not to embarrass them by extending a welcoming hand in return. Black people were forced to go to the back door, and if in a white person's house, could not take a seat. If a chair was sat in by a black, it had to be removed from the site, cleaned, or, quite likely, burned.

Mobs. Lynchings all over. A sad state of affairs. There was the day in 1940 when, about seventeen miles south of Lexington, near Goodman, Mississippi, a bereaved father, Sam Johnson, tried to talk robed KKK members into letting him finish burying his son, whose body had been found burned. They would not permit it. And they immediately threw the father into the son's open coffin, cradling his bloody head in his hands. The Klan members promptly buried him alive.

So times continued to be rough all over. But in the 1940s there were some hopeful signs. World War II helped the economy, for there were jobs for black mechanics and artisans, and some work was available for black people at the cotton gin. Seasonal work. Neighbors had houses to be built, wells to be dug, and walls to be made. And machinery to be repaired. Black people were prepared to do all those things. But none of these opportunities, even those spawned by war, applied to plantation people.

Conditions were not nearly as bad for us who were "standing renters" and homeowners as for so many others on plantations around us. "Oh, those terrible places! Those poor black tenants there," was heard often. Plantation people were in a whole world apart from ours.

The plantation that joined our place seemed so many worlds away. Our rented land was separated from that plantation only by a long, shallow gully thick with bush and small trees. Across that ditch was a different world. A frightful world, so very hard to imagine even during those times. The tenants on the plantation were croppers. That is, share-tenant croppers who paid one-half or more of their crops for the use of the land. Their animals were furnished by the planter (owner).

Almost everything was furnished by the owner of the land, so the tenants were "not even supposed" to get more than a very little for a year's work. And since they were entirely dependent on the owner of the plantation, the croppers were compelled to do almost whatever the planter demanded.

Tenants made verbal agreements with the landowner around the beginning or the end of the year. They then agreed to "sign" a contract that was enforced by law. Since most of the tenants were uneducated people with little or no knowledge of law, they easily signed away their rights and liberties, not knowing what they were doing. Tenants usually just made their "X" or touched the pen. Papa said that he watched the process "oh, so often," he told us.

These contracts definitely were not favorable to tenants. In addition, the interpretation of the agreements was completely in the hands of the planters and plantation owners. Planters would call upon the Lexington police to carry out the contracts when necessary.

The plight of the tenants can easily be seen in the following lease, which my father kept all these years. A tenant had asked him to explain this document:

> You the tenant further agrees that if you violate this contract, or neglects, or abandons or fails or (in Mr. ————'s judgment) violates this contract or fails to properly work or till the land early or at proper times, or in case you should become disabled or legally sick or hurt while working this land or should die during the term of your lease, or fails to gather or save the crops when made, or fails to pay the rents or advances made by me, whenever due, then in case of full possession of said premises, crops and improvements, in which event this contract may become void and canceled at my option, and all indebtedness by you for advances or rent shall at once become due and payable to me who may treat them as due and payable without further notice to you; and you hereby agree to surrender quietly and peacefully the possession of said premises to me at said time, in which event I am hereby authorized to transfer, sell or dispose of all property thereon you have any interest in, and in order to entitle me to do so, it shall not be necessary to give any notice of any failure or violation of this contract by you, the execution of this lease being sufficient notice of defalcation on the part of you, and shall be so construed between the parties hereto, any law, usage or custom to the contrary notwithstanding.

The struggles of those laborers on the plantations around us showed us firsthand about their tragic state. When croppers agreed to become tenants, the whole family came completely under domination of the landlord. And this was living hell for all of the families. Living hell.

One day after peddling vegetables in Tchula, I bought a small dictionary and a Superman comic book. I can see Tchula as if it were yesterday. I see the ten-cent store, the grocery, the white folks' coffee shop, and the bank that bonded the small community. From a distance, the little town seemed to blend into the cotton fields. Only the two-story school building for white children and the water tank rose above the wide landscape of soil and stalks. There was not much there in Tchula.

I was happy that day—I had bought something to read. A comic and a small dictionary. For us, reading was something special.

Reading made hard times and even our relationship with white people seem easier all around. Our parents and others on the Place read a lot. We all read a lot. Mama and Papa believed strongly in reading and exposure to a broad realm of knowledge. They were devout, lifelong learners who kept books around home on different subjects such as history, farming, opera, food, design, and architecture. Even my mother's education textbooks were family reading material. Newspapers were passed from family to family and hand to hand before they were discarded.

Our immediate family's favorite readings in those years were Du Bois's *Crisis*, Charles S. Johnson's *Opportunity*, and the *Chicago Daily Defender*. We had the chance to read because we were renters (and not croppers) during those times. Croppers had almost no such chance to read, and little exposure to the outside world.

Our books and reading were not limited to heavy or serious subjects, not by any means. The Archers read about and followed with keen interest the baseball career of the great Leroy "Satchel" Paige, who played with the Cleveland Indians as a relief pitcher, but whose achievements were limited primarily to black circuits. And just like American kids everywhere, we children exchanged lots of comic books.

I often think about the difference it may have made if plantation people had been permitted to go to school. If nothing else, just to learn to read. Being informed was, I suspect, the reason Papa became so very concerned about the disgraceful effect plantations had on the black people of Mississippi. He realized that everybody and everything suffered from plantation tenancy.

Our father realized that the church was an important community-building institution. The church went a long way toward helping us renters make it through tough times. But churches encountered major problems on the plantations, where often there were new congregations each year.

It was difficult to keep the interest of croppers in matters of the spirit. It stood to reason that without a fixed place to stay or a bond to the land, they would mainly be interested in the immediate needs of their families—eating, sleeping—and other day-to-day tasks. This posed a real serious problem for churches in those days; religion was not relevant, or so it often seemed to the plantation populace.

Ministers to an unstable plantation people were not the best prepared of their group. Only an intelligent person of the greatest devotion and sacrifice could be expected to spend his life in such an uninviting field. Preachers who were not wanted elsewhere drifted into plantation service. And, it was even worse if the landlord built the church or actually chose the minister.

If the church was built by the landowner, only those preachers who knew how to safeguard the interests of the planter were allowed to hold meetings on the premises. Their sermons were censored, and if they were found saying or doing anything that might cause dissatisfaction with things as they were, they would have to leave at once. Several field workers told my parents of planters and their representatives listening through windows of churches to find out what plantation preachers said to their congregations.

The baker, store owner, and professional people in the towns suffered from tenancy along with the teacher and preacher. Credit given to those unfortunate croppers was thought to mean ruin to business people. Tenants had nothing but their labor to sell, and if they were wandering types, lenders thought they would be left in a somewhat risky position. To make up for losses, money had to be loaned at a higher rate of interest. Goods were sold at higher prices to squeeze out those who were unable to take care of their obligations promptly.

Most plantation tenants, however, could get credit only in the commissaries of their landlords. They dared not purchase their necessities elsewhere. And, in the case of professional services given, creditors figured that they had a better chance of being paid back when their fees were collected through their customers' landlord. But the landlord doubled the cost because he figured that he had to make up for any time lost in assuming collection responsibilities. The whole economic system suffered from burdens put on a poor and unoffending people.

But all must remember that the condition of black people on plantations in the South in the 1930s and 1940s, bad as it was, was not insurmountable. Many blacks back then tended to rise from tenancy to ownership in spite of the difficulties that were involved.

Ownership of land actually increased at a faster rate for black farmers than for whites. My father and uncles and many others of that era were typical examples of such advancements.

There were definite stages of understanding in my life. For much of my youth, there was a "war of contradictions" in my mind, likely because of my young mind's presumptions that racial conditions did not exist or that they were at least bearable. I had always thought of the few whites I had met as "people, not oppressors." As a young child, out on the Place, I actually thought all the world was black. I saw only black people day after day. Later, I considered all people to be basically fair, all the same.

Somewhat later on, I naturally became skeptical. Then I became aware of feelings of white racial animosity toward me, while I was still at an early age. I also gradually realized that the situation was a lot more serious than we young folk were led to "know" out on the Place. There existed much more than whites' negative attitudes. Whites took direct action against black people, both psychologically and physically. But rarely against Indians or Asians who lived in Tchula. Or any other minority group. Just black people. I became increasingly hungry—no, starved—to learn more about this thing between black and white people.

Parchman, the state penitentiary located in Sunflower County, in those days was always filled to the brim. It seemed to me, even at my early age, that it was simply incredible for a person to be sentenced to one and a half years in jail for talking back to a merchant. And that a black person could be imprisoned for up to two years merely for "getting out of place." But it happened. And that's the way it was.

And I now realize that one did not have to live in Tchula to be emotionally and in every other way affected by the temper of the times.

Not too long ago I looked through some of my school notebooks about to be thrown away, and images came racing back. This is what I remembered: One morning I had finished my "peddling" and was riding Little Mare toward Tchula from the Gwin settlement. Little Mare was a special saddle horse given to me by Papa and Uncle Perry. As usual, I had been out selling fresh vegetables, from our garden out on the Place, to Tchula and Gwin people, the local hotels, and restaurants.

Little Mare. my good companion, was a witness to it all. That morning at about nine o'clock, we heard shotgun fire echoing through the town. A police car and another car roared down the road between Gwin and Tchula. Whites were shouting, whooping and hollering. This was not far from the Tchula Lake bridge and Guy Sharp's filling station. Two officers were in the police car and some unknown whites in the other. At the same time, two white policemen, each on horseback, were laughing as they frog-marched a handcuffed black man toward the jail house. One rider was on each side of the prisoner as he struggled on foot to keep up. I watched all this while keeping a tight rein on Little Mare. She seemed as alarmed as I was.

The black man was John Johnson, an attendant and general helper at another service station. I don't know what his "crime" was.

On another occasion, I remember seeing a black family being set upon by some white men brandishing rubber whips and—on tight leashes—snarling dogs. For no crime whatsoever. A most horrible and unforgettable experience. There were rumors, too, that black people were having gasoline poured on them as they walked down the road.

It may be difficult for those not around during those times to picture the atrocities that took place in towns in the Deep South, such as Tchula. I can so well remember, for example, Mrs. Price kneeling at the Mount Olive cemetery, her face contorted in grief before the yawning grave of her teenaged son, gunned down by unknown white men on his way to school a few days before.

Tchula, Mississippi, a Delta town with its five-and-dime and one bank and hardware store and icehouse, was a quintessential sleepy southern small town. However, Tchula was totally caught up in all the prejudices and racial fears that defined life in the region. But sometimes the reality did not hit home until I leafed through an old school notebook, and then remembered Little Mare and our ride that morning when we both flinched at the sound of shotguns—and the sight of John Johnson. The notebook was a kind of freeze-frame of Tchula, Mississippi.

Yes, these were very trying times for all of us black people in the rural South. But there still was that persisting hope and daily striving to eventually—and one by one—ignore, defy, and overwhelm the laws that confined us, and become free. I have many good memories of my experiences growing up in Tchula. After all, it was "home." And it's just human nature to want to look back kindly on a place of which you were once so much a part.

12 The Young Exile

 I still am not sure who she was. Some people thought they knew. But I was never sure. The woman wore a hood but was said to have removed it for a while to demonstrate her bravado as she rode through a black neighborhood in a Klan demonstration of power. She was known by her distinctive Klan array. What we did know for sure was that this woman was the local leader. And, under her leadership, the Ku Klux Klan had a long history of terrorizing black people and anyone else who disagreed with their point of view in Lexington, and in all Holmes County. The Klan, of course, advocated absolute white supremacy, and they were set on preventing any change from the subjugated conditions blacks found themselves in during the 1930s and 1940s.

Klan members were staunch racists and ruled by lynching and other violence. Race hatred and ethnic hatred formed the roots of their philosophy and action. They supported all Jim Crow laws with vigor. They apparently believed, also, that the old laws under slavery should be translated into new unwritten Jim Crow laws and customs to invalidate the Emancipation Proclamation. Thus, it is obvious the Klan's modus operandi was of the bully boy type—even with a lady in charge.

Papa and others, both black and white, often spoke of seeing a murdered black man hanging from a tree near the bridge close to where my family now lives. The man's body was left hanging for an entire day, a warning to the community. Everyone was sure this was the handiwork of the Klan. This happened in the 1930s, but the image lingered for years afterward.

At age sixteen, I had to deal with a gang called the Alley Cats—not the Klan—but the atmosphere of intimidation seemed much the same.

We all had gone to bed early that night, having finally decided during a lengthy family powwow that it would be best that I go to Detroit, Michigan, to stay with my father's niece for a while. I got little sleep that night. I lay awake that hot night thinking about lynchings, rumors of lynchings, and the lady KKK leader. She had taken off her hood! I shivered at the thought. I awakened that predawn morning in June 1945 and looked at my father and out the window into an impenetrable darkness, or so it seemed, just before the break of dawn. For some reason even the air appeared heavy and it was difficult to breathe. I continued to stare sightless into the ominous darkness for what seemed to be an eternity, although I realized it would soon be daylight.

For me, a sixteen-year-old who had never stayed away from home for more than a weekend with my grandmother (who lived about ten miles from us), this decision was traumatic. There were many tears shed by my mother and younger brothers and sisters. A lot of crying! And I can remember wondering if the decision that I go to Detroit for the summer would be harder on them than it might be on me.

My trip to Detroit was necessary because of the aforementioned Alley Cats, a gang of white youths who had begun harassing black youths. Similar to the groups that today are called skinheads, the Alley Cats were said to have killed a number of blacks, but they were mainly known throughout the county for calling black people derogatory names and occasionally physically abusing or harassing them. The Alley Cats were especially fond of bothering black kids going to and from the local black high school.

Most of the Alley Cats were no older than eighteen or nineteen, although some were obviously out of their teens. Many, we knew, carried weapons. Nevertheless, I was determined not to be intimidated by this group of thugs—although they were determined that we in the neighborhood would be cowed by their acts or taunts that went far beyond what we usually faced.

Black students who had to come through the town of Lexington to get to and from school would be stopped by the Alley Cats and told that they must follow only certain streets. After several classmates and I, including one girl, had been stopped several times for not following these directions, the Alley Cats decided to give us a graphic description of what they had done to others and would do to us if we disobeyed again.

Their litany of threats went like this: "We took one girl, stripped her, tied her hands behind her, and shot her in the back." The bravado escalated. "And remember the time we wrapped that old man in a gas-soaked mattress and burned him to death?"

"Yeah," another added, glancing at the female member of our group, "and take a look at this girl—I have killed two just like her."

Although I had not heard of any such lynchings actually happening under Alley Cat auspices, I could feel the hate emanating from this group and my only thought was how to survive these confrontations. There was no middle ground between us and the Alley Cats. We kids believed that we might indeed be attacked or killed, because this group was known to be harsh in their mission of instilling fear.

During the last meeting I had with this group I remember praying silently that I would not lose my nerve and show any sign of weakness. It was the inevitable, ultimate encounter: One of the Alley Cats was holding a gun. I remember staring directly into the eyes of the boy holding the gun that was pointed at me. Maybe this eye contact kept him from firing. I remember clearly the boy stepped back about six feet. "Stand away from me!" he said.

It was as if I was someone else looking at myself.

Silence. No one moved. After what seemed like hours, but that could only have been several seconds, one of the older Alley Cats suddenly said, "We can get them if they come this way again. They better go straight home and never come this way again. Let's go home." They turned away, and were gone. That day, we walked home extra fast. After this encounter, all of us began to think of ourselves as real soldiers in a daily game of war.

My classmates and I considered ourselves lucky that time. But our worry was not just for ourselves, but also for the smaller children and the rest of our families. We had decided we must meet fire with fire, and our families were dreading that outright war would break out. Because of this possible danger to the rest of my family, at first I refused to leave for Detroit. I was the brave young warrior, but Papa knew I was a vulnerable one. The Alley Cats were known to prey on one family member to intimidate the rest of a family.

At about this time our barn burned under suspicious circumstances in the middle of the night. The flames killed King, Papa's best mule at the time. Perhaps the barn burned because of spontaneous combustion caused by moldering hay, but nobody knows. Traditionally, burning down someone's barn was a common form of both threat and revenge. For this reason, I, too, decided to carry a gun.

My parents did not want me to kill or get killed. Detroit was the solution. Because of their anguish I finally agreed to leave Lexington at least for that summer, following my senior year in high school. It was an agonizing decision for me.

But because none of us bowed to their intimidation, and because the leader of the group was himself soon killed, the Alley Cats were disbanded.

"One thing for sure," Papa said, "is that we must not hand our heads on a platter to 'Mr. Charlie.' " (Handing one's head to Mr. Charlie was the equivalent of giving up completely to the white majority.)

Father made it known that it was as good a time as ever for that summer to become the "dawn of civil rights in America." This was the middle of the great black migration from the rural South to the big cities in the North, and apparently I was to be part of it. Nevertheless, Papa was still of the firm conviction that a lot of productive things could happen if young people would become more interested in their own backyards. Why not remain in Mississippi, and expand from there? "And not fear the unknown," he often lectured. Sometimes I listened with only half an ear. I was sixteen; why send me to Detroit?

In our opinion we were not poor. The smokehouses and pantries and jars and garden were full of food. The orchard cellars and meat bins too. If we were poor, no one told us. We nearly always had some new clothes for the new school year.

As kids and young adults, we measured time by the seasons. And our outlooks were set by our daily tasks and the ripening of fruits and vegetables. We fished in the creeks and set hooks when the water was rising. Hooks were set for catfish and sometimes freshwater eels. When high waters went down after the spring rains, we fished in water holes in the swamps and low grounds by "mudding." This meant stirring the mud up in the bottom of the hole with a hoe or with our feet. The fish would come to the top for oxygen and we could scoop them up with a homemade net or our hands.

All of us boys were excellent tree climbers, and some would be invited by hunters to go on night hunts. Those invited would climb up and shake down tree animals. For some, this was fun. For others like me, it was not. I did not enjoy seeing the quarry tumble down out of the tree, to the joy of the hounds, to death.

Farm work was full and heavy year-round. Although schoolwork always came first, children could expect teachers to give short home-work assignments during planting and harvest times. So we continued to learn even outside the schoolroom and during the long "vacations" between school terms. We were always taught that as long as we continued to learn, we were not poor in any sense of the word.

There were always yards to sweep, stove wood to cut, stack, and bring in, and water to draw from the cistern and springs.

There were also vegetables and fruits to gather and younger children to tend. The girls filled the lamps with kerosene and cleaned the lamps' chimneys.

Every boy and some girls had dogs. Dogs were constant companions for most. Dogs were playmates and were also for hunting squirrels, rabbits, raccoons, opossums, and similar small game. Our family had Tip, "the smartest dog the world," and Uncle Nick had Collie, "the largest and the blackest dog in the world." Boys usually were about twelve years old before they were allowed to hunt alone with dogs.

One of the most exciting times of the year for us youngsters was when redhouse sucker fish were running. Then young adults and boys would go down below the hill to the creeks and stand in the swift water at night with a flashlight and gig the suckers as they swam upstream on their yearly pilgrimage. Suckers were fearsome fighters, and the meat was delicious. It had to be slashed in thin strips so that the tiny bones could be well cooked. Most everyone was afraid of getting fish bones stuck in his or her throat. Every family had a story to tell about fish bone problems, but this never diminished our zeal for fishing.

One reason kids never complained about hard work was because it was a "way of life." The everyday work was expected. We knew that hard work was necessary to "make it." And also because grown-ups and young adults always worked harder than we did.

Most parents in those days were stern disciplinarians and punished severely if children misbehaved. Our father never touched us, but our mother, "Miss Eva," took long, flexible peach tree switches to the boys when necessary. She "wore us out!"

And we were family. A family that extended throughout the whole farming community. One big warm loving family that pitched in to do what had to be done for survival. All of this made wonderful childhood memories for us all. And all of this helped to keep us from feeling poor. Mostly, though, it was the bounty of the land, from pecans and peanuts to watermelons to hay, that kept us from want.

At times we had as many as two hundred chickens that were of hen and frying size. Hens would sit on the eggs and hatch more chickens. We had only a few ducks. Maybe ten to twelve at one time. We occasionally sold one. Sometimes we sold a pair.

We still talk about blackberries the size of quarters, dark sweet blueberries as big as thumbnails. And deep red strawberries the size of golf balls. Tangy and delicate raspberries. Juicy peaches and crisp, aromatic apples.

Who could forget the homemade preserves? The putting up, canning, of preserves and pickles. And the making of special pies and cakes. Some years Papa made peach brandy and some blackberry wine. He would often offer a glass of one or the other to special truck garden customers. We fondly remember the wooden bucket with ever present dipper, full of shade or creek-cooled spring water or well water for drinking.

In the fall we gathered wild persimmons softened by a frost. We also picked mulberries, which made delicious cobblers. And there were those wild blueberries . . .

Our farm sales and peddling went a long way toward individual and group survival during a time when state welfare services for black people were limited. Our farm products also helped other farmers and townspeople bypass merchants and stay out of debt at town stores. Our efforts helped, too, when there was a "bad year" on the farm for us and for others. Most of the time bad years were caused by the weather and boll weevils, equally damaging to all.

The truck crops took lots of afterschool hoeing, planting, pruning, and the like. The whole family worked as a team. Some of us sweeping down the rows, another weeding, another planting and trimming, and another one of us carrying off the underbrush and trash. Papa or I usually did all the plowing.

The truck garden was the site of great family pleasures for us all. Yes, truckpatches were indeed the real "fun" aspect of making ends meet, working as a team, and helping others in the community. How could we ever think of ourselves as poor?

Our close affiliation with two local churches also enriched our lives. I remember that just down the street from Mama Lucy's we went to the Berean Church for Sunday school, and sometimes for church too. Where some of us were baptized and married. It was close to Saint Paul's, the Church of God and Christ, where we often went for Sunday night services. Saints Industrial and Literary School was founded under the auspices of St. Paul's.

It is hard to believe the changes that took place during those years. Many have been good. But not before my parents joined with other black families in demanding changes. Of course, a real treat for the Archer family was to finally have indoor plumbing.

The Archer family is still there. Some other families are not. Tchula and Lexington will always be part of me. No matter how far I stray,

Holmes County will always be home. How horribly and how wonderfully it treated me. Some of the people I cherish most in the world live within its borders. Growing up black in Mississippi taught us to appreciate the big things in life, such as the importance of the family, the church, and the community as a whole.

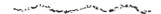

We owned five cows during those days. The one I was supposed to milk was named Simplicity—Simp for short. She was a jersey, dusky with big udders and long, rubbery teats that I was to milk at 5:00 A.M. and 6:00 P.M. Properly milked, Simp could supply about three quarts to over a gallon of high-butterfat milk a day. Good, fresh milk, soon to be cooled in the spring. The problem was, I never did really learn how to milk. It was a matter of motivation—I kind of thought that milking was a girl's chore.

Simp, a creature of exceptional gentleness, was part of the small herd that I was to help milk and supervise. She came by her name because, with sweet simplicity, she wandered off occasionally from her designated pasture, even though it abounded with sorghum and crimson clover. She would jump a fence, or sidle through it, and search for grass that was not only greener but tastier.

Trouble usually came the next milking. Residues of dandelion and "bitter weed" turned up. The milk had a bitter flavor, not the sweet kind from sorghum and clover. The cow was never able to be conditioned to stay pastured with the rest of the herd. But I always admired her for her wayward, independent ways.

Those were days on the farm I fondly remember. Simp's gentle rebelliousness was especially appealing to a sixteen-year-old boy far from home. I thought of her often during the summer of my exile in Detroit. My new friends, sophisticated city kids, Tiger fans, would ask: Is life down there in Mississippi bad? Yes, sometimes very bad, I would reply. Are your folks real poor?

No, we were not poor.

Appendix: Helpful Resources for Research on Black American History

REPORTS OF THE U.S. BUREAU OF THE CENSUS

Fourteenth Census of the United States Population Taken in the Year 1920. Prepared under the supervision of William C. Hunt, chief statistician for population. (Composition and Characteristics of the Population by States.) Washington, D.C.: U.S. Government Printing Office, 1932. P. 535.

Negroes in the United States 1920–32. Prepared under the supervision of Z. R. Pettet, chief statistician for agriculture, and by Charles E. Hall, specialist in negro statistics. (Negro Churches—Number of Churches, Membership, Number and Value of Church Edifices, Debt Expenditures, and Sunday School, by Denominations, by States, 1926.) Washington, D.C.: U.S. Government Printing Office, 1935. Pp. 536, 544, 550.

Fifteenth Census of the United States: 1930, Census of Agriculture. The Negro Farmer in the United States. (Farms Operated by Negroes—Number, Acreage, and Value of Specified Classes of Farm Property, by States and Counties, 1930.) Washington, D.C.: U.S. Government Printing Office, 1933. Pp. 56–84.

Fifteenth Census of the United States: 1930, Agriculture, Part 2—The Southern States. Prepared under the supervision of William Lane Austin, chief statistician for agriculture. (Reports by States, with Statistics for Counties and a Summary for the United States, Agriculture—Mississippi.) Washington, D.C.: U.S. Government Printing Office, 1932. Pp. 1050–51, 1056–57, 1062–63, 1070–71, 1126–27.

Fifteenth Census of the United States: 1930, Population, Alabama—Missouri. Prepared under the supervision of Leon E. Truesdell, chief statistician for population. (Reports by States, Showing the Composition and Characteristics of the Population for Counties, Cities, and Townships or Other Minor Civil Divisions.) Washington, D.C.: U.S. Government Printing Office, 1932. Vol. 3, part 1, pp. 1265, 1269, 1273, 1283, 1289, 1295.

Religious Bodies: 1936. Summary and Detailed Tables. (Negro Churches— Number of Churches, Membership, by Denominations—Mississippi.) Washington, D.C.: U.S. Government Printing Office, 1941. Vol. 1, pp. 864, 865, 884, 885.

OTHER RESOURCES

AFRO-AMERICAN RESEARCH CENTER
Founders Library
Howard University
Washington, D.C. 20059

THE ANACOSTIA NEIGHBORHOOD MUSEUM
Smithsonian Institution
2405 Martin Luther King Avenue, S.E.
Washington, D.C. 20020

CARTER G. WOODSON CENTER
1401 14th Street, N.W.
Washington, D.C. 20005

EUDORA WELTY PUBLIC LIBRARY
Jackson, Mississippi 39201

FAIRFAX COUNTY PUBLIC LIBRARY SYSTEM
Annandale, Virginia 22003

THE FANNIE BOOKER MUSEUM
Tchula Road
Lexington, Mississippi 39095

FLOREWOOD RIVER PLANTATION
P.O. Box 680
Greenwood, Mississippi 38930

FREDERICK DOUGLASS MEMORIAL AND HISTORICAL ASSOCIATION
14th and W Streets, S.E.
Washington, D.C. 20020

THE GEORGE WASHINGTON CARVER MUSEUM
Tuskegee University
College Street
Tuskegee, Alabama 36088

THE HOLLIS BURKE FURKE LIBRARY
Tuskegee University
College Street
Tuskegee, Alabama 36088

THE *LEXINGTON ADVERTISER* ARCHIVES
"On the Square"
Lexington, Mississippi 39095

LEXINGTON PUBLIC LIBRARY
Lexington, Mississippi 39095

LIBRARY OF CONGRESS
Washington, D.C. 20540

THE MISSISSIPPI AGRICULTURE, FORESTRY, AND NATIONAL
    AGRICULTURAL AVIATION MUSEUM
1150 Lakeland Drive
Jackson, Mississippi 39216

MISSISSIPPI DEPARTMENT OF ARCHIVES AND HISTORY
Archives and Library Division
P.O. Box 571
Jackson, Mississippi 39205

MOORLAND–SPINGARN RESEARCH CENTER
Howard University
Washington, D.C. 20059

NORTHERN VIRGINIA COMMUNITY COLLEGE LIBRARY
Alexandria Campus
3001 North Beauregard Street
Alexandria, Virginia 22311

SMITH ROBERSON BLACK CULTURAL CENTER
1968 Wingfield Circle
Jackson, Mississippi 39302

TRACE PARK
Route 1, Box 254
Belden, Mississippi 38873

Index

African folk heritage, 72
African Methodist Episcopal Church, 65
Alcorn State University, 20, 113
Alley Cats gang, 141–43
Ambrose Vocational High School, 111–16, 118, 125, 129–30
    graduation from, 119, 121
Anderson, Marian, 117–18
Army, U.S., 24–26
Asians, 137

Balance Due community, 13, 104–5, 110
Banneker, Benjamin, 38
Baptist churches, 5–6, 65
Barns, 47
    burning of, 143
Baseball, 135
Berean Church, 146
Births, 94–97, 104
Black Puritans, 7
Blacksmith shop, 4, 48
Blues, 118, 121
Books, 135
Bush, George, 99

Candle making, 48
Cars, 6, 10
Carver, George Washington, 27, 38
Catholic University of America, 113
Cattle, 59
    butchering, 43, 99
    milking, 11, 147
Cattle drives, 22
Chain gangs, 68–70
Chicago, 53, 126
    migration to, 14, 105
Chicago Daily Defender, 16, 135

Chickens, 42, 145
Chores, 11–12, 144
Christmas traditions, 46–47
Churches, 48, 64–67, 70–72, 106–9, 146
    on plantations, 135–36
    schools in, 44, 74, 108, 111–13
Civilian Conservation Corps (CCC), 8, 105
Civil rights, 15, 40, 67–68, 143
    imprisonment of protesters for, 68–69
    during Reconstruction era, 83
    white supporters of, 43
Civil War, 57, 82, 85
Clark, Clenton L., 71
Coal oil, 90–91
Comic books, 134, 135
Community, sense of, 101–2, 109
Conjuring, 80–81
Cooking, 7, 38–39, 55–58, 145, 146
    for Christmas, 46, 47
    for church suppers, 65–66
Corn bread, 56–57
Corporal punishment, 20
Cotton, 11, 45, 47, 48, 59, 74, 102, 116–17
Crisis, 135

Daughters of the American Revolution, 117
Davis, Jim, 115
Davis, Mrs. N. Thomas, 115
DDT, 93–94
Deaths, 94, 104
    early, 99–100
    from influenza, 98
    statistics on, 88
Democratic Party, 105

Dental care, lack of, 91–92
Detroit, 105, 141, 143, 147
Dogs, 144
"Dog trot" houses, 4
Domestic service, 54
Du Bois, W. E. B., 135

Education, 26, 48
    civil rights and, 68
    denied to black children, 44
    outdoors on farm, 122, 123, 144
    See also Schools
Emancipation Proclamation, 140
Equality, fight for. *See* Civil rights
Erosion, 7–8

Farm Home Administration, 14
Farm Journal, 26–27
Farm Security Administration (FSA), 14,
    103
Field work, 8, 12, 26, 74, 82, 144
    missing school for, 20, 117
Fishing, 144, 145
Food. *See* Cooking
Forced labor, 62–64

Games, 14
Great Depression, 16, 42, 51–54, 62–64,
    72
Greenwood (Miss.), 58, 76, 79, 108

Hay crop, 60
Health conditions, 87–91, 97–100
    for births, 94–97
    on plantations, 8
Hearthside cooking, 38
Hexes, 80
Hogs, 42, 99
    killing of, 4–5, 43
Hollywood movies, images of blacks in,
    63
Hoover, Herbert, 62–63
Hoppers, 47
Horses, 10, 11, 45
Houseparties, 121

Houses, 6–7, 42, 46, 52
    antebellum, 36
    built by FSA, 15
    "clean space" at back door of, 13–14
    decorated for Christmas, 46
    "dog trot," 4
    and health conditions, 88
    in Lexington, 130
    and outbuildings, 47
Hunting, 24, 144

Ice houses, 28, 65
Indiana University, 113
Indians, 21, 103, 137
Influenza epidemics, 89, 98
Insect infestations, 92–93
Intermarriage, 78
    with Indians, 21

Jackson (Miss.), 58, 61
Jim Crow laws, 39, 84, 110, 125, 140
Johnson, Charles S., 135
Johnson, Lonnie, 52
June bugs, 9

King, B. B., 118
Knocking, 20
Kudzu, 7–8
Ku Klux Klan, 19, 32–35, 49, 79, 83, 84,
    133, 140–41

Lexington (Miss.), 13, 16, 18, 19, 21–23,
    28, 53, 61, 71, 95, 96, 99, 101–3, 105,
    109–10, 146
    churches in, 65
    civil rights protests in, 69
    houses in, 130
    Klan in, 140–41
    racism in, 124–26, 132, 141–43
    schools in, 106, 111–19
Lincoln, Abraham, 105, 118
Logging, 27–28
Louis, Joe, 105
Lynchings, 16, 32, 40, 43, 79, 83, 125, 133,
    140–42

McCoy, Elijah, 38
Manufacturing, employment in, 53
Meats, 53
 smoking of, 4–5
Medical care. *See* Health conditions
Medicinal plants, 21
Memphis, 53, 105
Migration to North, 14, 101, 105, 110, 126–27, 143
Milking, 11, 147
Mississippi State University, 113
Molasses mill, 46
Morgan, Garrett, 38
Moses, Sorphonia, 119
Mound Bayou (Miss.), 27
Mount Olive community, 19–24, 26, 55, 73, 85
 Ku Klux Klan in, 32
Mount Olive Church, 30–32, 64–66, 70
 school in, 74, 111–13
Mount Zion Baptist Church, 106–9
Mules, 10–11, 45, 131, 132
Music
 blues, 118, 121
 in church, 71
Mustard plasters, 95–96, 99

Newspapers, 16, 135
New York City, 126
 returning soldiers from World War I in, 25, 26

Opportunity, 135
Orchards, 5, 6, 60
Outhouses, 42, 47, 104
Oxen, 22

Paige, Leroy "Satchel," 135
Parchman State Penitentiary, 137
Peddling, 17–18, 51, 134, 138, 146
Place, the, 3–14, 16, 23, 26, 41–60, 62–63, 94, 107, 111, 119–21, 124, 135, 137
Plantations, 46, 49, 75–76
 black women on, 54
 forced labor on, 63, 64

living conditions on, 8–9, 15, 52
 migration from, 105
 during slavery, 1–2, 78, 84–85, 110
 tenancy on, 62, 133–37
Plowing, 10, 11, 45, 131–32
Polio, 89
Polk, Almeta Coleman, 113–15
Poll taxes, 125, 127
Potato hacks, 4
Pottery, 48
Poverty, 52–54, 61, 104, 105
 on plantations, 8–9, 15, 133–34
Progressive Farmer, 27

Quilt making, 116

Racism, 124–29, 132–33, 137, 141–43
 "rules" of, 5, 16, 39–40. *See also* Jim Crow laws; Segregation
 violence of, *see* Ku Klux Klan; Lynching
Railroad work, 28
Reading, 135
Reconstruction, 32, 73, 77–79
Religion. *See* Churches
Remedies, folk, 81–82, 90–91
Republican Party, 105
Rice with walnuts and cider, recipe for, 39
Roosevelt, Franklin D., 65, 105
Rose Hill Church, 70, 128
 school in, 44, 108, 111
Rote learning, 20

Saint Paul's Church of God and Christ, 146
Saints Industrial and Literary School, 113, 146
Schools, 108, 111–19, 122
 budget cuts for, 105–6
 and farm work, 144
 one-room, 19–20, 74, 111
Segregation, 16, 39–40, 52, 78, 79, 84, 109, 124–28
 of armed forces, 110

"Separate but equal" doctrine, 112, 125
Sharecroppers, 8–9, 52, 62, 63, 75, 82, 117, 133–37
Slavery, 1–2, 19, 31, 46, 52, 54, 78–80, 83–85, 103, 109–10, 128, 140
  education unlawful during, 116
  end of, 5, 54–55, 57, 82
  medical treatment during, 98
  separation of families during, 85
Smokehouses, 4–5, 47
Snakes, 41–44
  hexes using, 80–81
  in Mount Olive Church, 30–32
Supreme Court, U.S., 112

Talbot, Dorothy Hamilton, 116
Tchula (Miss.), 3, 13, 19, 21–23, 31, 36, 38, 61, 99, 101, 103, 134–35, 146
  blues houseparties in, 121
  churches in, 65, 70, 106–9
  during Depression, 53
  jail in, 49
  Klan in, 32–35
  racism in, 126, 129, 138–39
  segregation in, 40
  weather in, 51, 59
  See also Place, the

Tenancy. See Sharecroppers
Townsend, Dewitt, 119
Trees, 43
  climbing, 144
Truck crops, 48, 51, 59, 146
Tuberculosis, 87–88
Tuskegee Institute, 27, 106

Urban poverty, 53

Vicksburg (Miss.), 22
Vocational training, 111–12
Voting, 67, 105, 129–30
  blacks prevented from, 15, 63, 69, 127

Wages, 53, 62
Walnut cider rice, recipe for, 39
Washington, Booker T., 27, 116
Washington, George, 118
Water supply, 42, 104
Whipping of slaves, 1–2
Williams, Gransbill, 69
Works Progress Administration (WPA), 105
World War I, 19, 21, 24–26
World War II, 110, 133